Helion & Company Limited
Unit 8 Amherst Business Centre
Budbrooke Road
Warwick
CV34 5WE
England
Tel. 01926 499 619
Email: info@helion.co.uk
Website: www.helion.co.uk
Twitter: @helionbooks
https://helionbooks.wordpress.com/

Text © David Baker 2024
Photographs © as individually credited
Colour Artwork © Jean-Marie Guillou and Goran Sudar

Cover image: A Lockheed P-80B from the 1st FG, representative of a type supreme in early postwar years of the US Air Force. (USAF)

Designed and typeset by Mach 3 Solutions (www.mach3solutions.co.uk)
Cover design Paul Hewitt, Battlefield Design (www.battlefield-design.co.uk)

Every reasonable effort has been made to trace copyright holders and to obtain their permission for the use of copyright material. The author and publisher apologise for any errors or omissions in this work, and would be grateful if notified of any corrections that should be incorporated in future reprints or editions of this book.

ISBN: 978-1-804513-75-0

British Library Cataloguing-in-Publication Data
A catalogue record for this book is available from the British Library

All rights reserved. No part of this publication may be reproduced, stored in a retrieval system, or transmitted, in any form, or by any means, electronic, mechanical, photocopying, recording or otherwise, without the express written consent of Helion & Company Limited.

We always welcome receiving book proposals from prospective authors.

CONTENTS

Abbreviations and acronyms	2
Preface	2
Introduction	3
1 Holding the Peace	3
2 Building for War	12
3 Lions and Lambs	22
4 Fighters For The Force	29
5 Roles and Responsibilities	63
Appendix: Stalled and Transient Projects	70
A Note on Sources	83
Bibliography	84
About the Author	84

Note: In order to simplify the use of this book, all names, locations and geographic designations are as provided in *The Times World Atlas*, or other traditionally accepted major sources of reference, as of the time of described events.

ABBREVIATIONS AND ACRONYMS

AAF	Army Air Forces	GDP	Gross Domestic Product
ADC	Air Defense Command	GE	General Electric
AF	Air Force	GOR	General Operational Requirement
AFA	(US) Air Force Association	hr	Hour
AFB	Air Force Base	IFF	identification friend or foe
AI	aircraft interception	MDAP	Mutual Defense Assistance Programme
AMC	Air Materiel Command	MX	Materiel Experimental
ANG	Air National Guard	NAA	North American Aviation
ATC	Air Training Command, or	NACA	National Advisory Committee for Aeronautics
ATC	Air Transport Command	NATO	North Atlantic Treaty Organization
ConAC	Continental Air Command	NFS	Night Fighter Squadron
DX	Direct Experimental	RAF	Royal Air Force
ETO	European Theatre of Operations	SAC	Strategic Air Command
F(AW)G	Fighter (All Weather) Group	TAC	Tactical Air Command
F(AW)S	Fighter (All Weather) Squadron	UN	United Nations
FAI	*Fédération Aéronautique Internationale*	USAAC	US Army Air Corps
FFAR	Folding Fin Aerial Rocket	USAAF	United States Army Air Forces
FG	Fighter Group	USAF	US Air Force
FS	Fighter Squadron	USAFE	United States Air Force(s) Europe
FW	Fighter Wing	VHB	very heavy bombardment
gal	Gallon (US)		

PREFACE

This is the first in a series of 15 volumes covering the story of US land-based and naval air power during the Cold War between 1945 and 1990. The series is divided into five separate chronological periods, each with three dedicated volumes subjectively aligned with significant developments in the history of American combat aircraft and US air power.

The intention is to provide a broad, spectral analysis of the origin, design, development and evolution of US Air Force combat aircraft as well as the political, industrial, design and manufacturing base from which they, and their variants, were developed. The volumes provided for each period, covering fighters and bombers, together present a story of US military air power.

For reasons of space, these volumes cannot provide an exhaustive history of each aircraft, that information being available in a wide range of published sources, including books, magazines and electronic archives. Instead, they integrate all those separate elements which supported and enabled the aviation and aerospace industries to produce the technologies underpinning the evolution of US combat aircraft throughout the Cold War.

Readers will note that this first volume also covers the US aviation industry at large between 1945 and 1949, providing a base upon which to explain why decisions were made and how those affected the designs and prototypes produced. The main chapters explore the decisions made at a political, technical and industrial level and include a description of the fighters flown and brought to operational status. It also provides information on who controlled the decisions and how the leadership viewed the national defence agenda.

An appendix describes speculative projects by type, some of which were flown but never entered production, while tables provide the characteristics and performance data for the fighters that equipped the US Air Force and the Air National Guard in this four-year period, as well as for the experimental and prototype aircraft listed in the appendix.

Volume 2 covers bombers and Volume 3 the emerging era of post-war naval aviation, following the same general format but the extensive description of the impact of demobilisation and downsizing of the industry and the years of fiscal constraint contained in this volume will not be repeated there. Instead, opening chapters of Volume 2 describe the origin and evolution of national air policy, long-range bombing and the creation of strategic air power in the US Air Force before covering operational and experimental bomber types.

Successive, volumes will cover fighters and bombers in the Korean War (1950–1953), before moving to the period during which the century-series appeared and supersonic combat aircraft became operational (1954–1960). The series then moves to the period when much change occurred before and during the Vietnam War (1961–1975) before covering the closing years of the Cold War when stealth and advanced combat systems were introduced (1976–1990).

Operational histories will be introduced only when they pertain to the development of fighter and bomber aircraft of the periods covered, emphasis being placed instead on the technical and engineering development of the different aircraft types. There are already copious sources for readers to obtain highly detailed accounts of operational histories. As with this first book, successive volumes will also include failed types either proposed and never built or brought to experimental evaluation without series production.

I wanted to write this series because I felt that the story of American air power had usually been defined through either the type histories of aircraft involved or the personal reminiscences of pilots and aircrew. Nowhere was there a single source of reference that brought it all together, with coverage of the aviation industry, the political base upon which significant decisions were made and the technical choices available to manufacturers and design teams. By integrating the story of these aspects with the aircraft in general, I wanted to provide something different, through coverage that also included the technical, engineering, industrial, political and strategic decisions that both shaped the US Air Force and the way it evolved throughout the Cold War.

David Baker
England, 2024

INTRODUCTION

The single-seat fighter and the long-range bomber would be key assets in establishing global air power during the Cold War. Independent since 1947, the US Air Force emerged from a period of demobilisation and contraction, imposed by greatly reduced defence budgets, further compromised by a degree of uncertainty as to just what it should be based upon and what equipment it should have.

Industry had already provided new technology, both in manufacturing materials and fabrication techniques, and the major aviation companies were not short on ideas. These would serve both the more conventional designs involving reciprocating engines and rotating propellers and newer aircraft powered by jet propulsion. Launched in the UK and Germany, the jet engine was very quickly exploited by the United States before the end of the Second World War, although this would be only one of several new capabilities.

Innovative designs provided a wide range of innovative concepts, providing high-speed/high-altitude flight, range-extension, tailless and blended wing-body shapes and mixed-propulsion involving reciprocating and jet engines, jet engines and rocket motors and aircraft combining both propeller-driven and jet propulsion on the same wing. Fighters were pushed close to the speed of sound and bombers acquired longer range, compensating for fuel-thirsty jet engines by increased aerodynamic efficiency and reduced drag.

In 1945 the constrained capabilities of a post-war air force were unable to stand up a capable air combat strength equal to the challenges of an increasingly hostile world, in which autocratic states threatened democratic countries across the globe. By 1949 the US Air Force had transformed the air power dynamic, establishing a doctrine of deterrence through the capacity for dropping large numbers of atomic bombs on any belligerent country anywhere on Earth.

That job was bequeathed to a new generation of jet-powered, intercontinental bombers tasked with preventing war through a new strategic air arm equipped with a rapidly expanding force carrying greater strike power than any fielded heretofore. Reliance on a strategic bomber force to deter aggression and suppress belligerent states would form the core of air power for the next decade, until tactical air applications achieved new, high-level status during the Vietnam War.

The fighters described in this book were first-generation designs powered by jet engines and incorporating radical concepts such as swept wings, equipped with rockets and missiles for air defence and ground attack. There were many designs funded and brought to flight status but rejected for one or other reasons. They formed the basis upon which derivatives of those that were made operational preceded the design of second-generation fighters which would emerge during the Korean War, that story being told in a later volume.

The story of this dynamic introduction to the jet age is told in the first three volumes of this history of US Air Force air power doctrine, a narrative forming the basis upon which the service adapted and changed to meet new requirements as challenges arose throughout the 45 years of the Cold War.

1
HOLDING THE PEACE

When the Second World War ended in September 1945 the demobilisation of US armed services was already in full swing. At that date there were 12.2 million military personnel in uniform of which 5.88 million were in the Army, somewhat fewer than 2.4 million in the Air Forces, 3.38 million in the Navy and 474,700 in the Marines and a further 86,000 in the Coast Guard. Of that total, approximately 7.6 million were abroad and in the preceding months they had begun preparations for the Allied assault on mainland Japan. But that was before the capitulation. By 30 June 1947 only 1.5 million remained in uniform and, according to some, the nation's defences were reduced to 'near impotency'.

Pressure on the national economy was great, as industry turned swords into ploughshares and skilled labour was offloaded from the factories at a frightening pace. Aircraft manufacturers struggled to stay in business and competition was fierce to get government contracts. Many existing projects were terminated, others with some promise were cancelled, existing orders were rescinded and the industry faced a near calamitous situation, some companies going under where once they could have survived. There was still a need for national defence, however and a few fighter projects such as the P-80, the F-86 and the F-84 had appeared. Operational deployment would underpin that requirement. But there were also some new development contracts to be had and the lean years of 1945–1949 would be quickly followed by a call-to-arms at the start of the Korean War.

The four years that began toward the end of 1945 were a period during which a range of new technologies in design and manufacturing were applied, if not perfected, and the pressures of the emerging Cold War injected new incentive by way of aggressive communist practices in Eastern Europe, not least the Berlin Airlift of 1948–49. A situation for which the US military was ill-prepared because of extensive demobilisation of the Army Air Force (AAF), which had begun long before the end of the war. Plans for that were being laid in 1943, by which date Germany's defeat was over-optimistically believed to be imminent followed by the defeat of Japan shortly thereafter. The need for demobilisation was driven by a desire to reduce the government war budget as quickly as possible, while simultaneously maintaining the armed forces necessary to defeat the enemy.

The first demobilisation plan had been made public on 31 July 1943. But it was complex because America was simultaneously fighting two wars, neither of which had certainty of completion by a specified date, with that against Japan to some extent determined by the timing of the defeat of Nazi Germany. Redeployment from the European Theatre of Operations (ETO) to the Pacific Theatre of Operations (PTO) would be one part of a phased demobilisation. In July 1943 the earliest possible end to the war against Germany was deemed to be 1 September 1944, an unlikely possibility given the task ahead, confidence having been encouraged by the eviction of

German and Italian forces from North Africa, with the invasion of Sicily in July 1943.

In February 1944 the Tompkins Demobilization Plan provided structural projections for how forces would be redeployed to Japan after the defeat of Germany, which was expected much earlier than actually achieved. Nevertheless, experience with chaotic scenes during previous periods of mass demobilisation – in 1865 after the American Civil War and 1918 after the First World War – made the advantage of early preparations self-evident. The Tompkins plan envisaged that the AAF would have 154 groups in the ETO and North Africa with 112 groups moved to the Far East for the war against Japan. Throughout the period of redeployment the AAF had to set up and administer facilities, stations and bases in the United States for processing the vast number of men and women demobilised and returned to civilian life, as well as coordinating those remaining in service and being assigned to other duties to maintain minimum defence requirements.

In 1941 General Henry Harley Arnold became Chief of the Army Air Forces and played a major part in structuring it for wartime operations, influencing the way the independent US Air Force would be established in 1947. (USAF)

Personnel levels in the AAF peaked at 2,411,294 in March 1944 from which it began to slowly decline, falling to 1,992,960 in September 1945, the month in which the surrender of Japan was signed on the deck of the USS *Missouri*. Demobilisation had been under the Army Service Forces which had 22 centres capable of processing 300,000 personnel a month. In September, the backlog of those eligible stood at 500,000 and the figure was expected to remain the same in the following month. By 1 October the AAF had separated 304,564 personnel and there was no backlog.

Equally impressive was the demobilisation of units. The peak strength of 243 groups in March 1945 had been reduced to 218 groups at the time of the Japanese surrender and to 109 by the end of the year, a reduction of 50 percent in four months. But the effective loss in personnel strength was very much greater. The procedure for demobilisation began first with the most experienced people with the greatest number of flying hours, as measured by 'points' to which a return to civilian life was given priority as acknowledgement of their service record. With the most expert and experienced getting home first, the capacity of units to carry out their duties was reduced in efficiency and in effectiveness. But the cascade of demobilisation continued throughout the following year and that had a measurable effect on morale, damaging that vital ingredient, the 'spirit' of a fighting force.

In October 1945, General Henry 'Hap' Arnold received a letter from Major General St Clair Street from the Continental Air Force asserting that 'we will have soon reached a point, if it has not been reached, at which the Army Air Forces can no longer be considered anything more than a symbolic instrument of National Defense', adding that 'a potpourri of warm bodies' was no substitute for an air force. Behind which were differing views at the Department of War and in Congress as to the type of armed services which would be required after the defeat of Japan, with universal acceptance that there would have to be a considerable reduction in the size of individual air forces.

In January 1946 the AAF had 89 groups, reducing to 81 in February, 71 in March, 65 in April, 60 in May, 54 in June and 52 in July, where it remained. At the end of the war with Japan the AAF had 1,895 installations, down from a peak of 2,252 in December 1943. The majority were in the United States but by VE Day at the beginning of May 1945 these had been cut from 1,133 to 429 and that included all the auxiliary fields supporting the prime stations and bases. On those installations in Europe the AAF had 24,000 spare aircraft engines, 238,000 tons of technical supplies, 12,000 special purpose vehicles and more than 466,000 tons of bombs and ammunition.

Keeping Stock

By 1 January 1946, the United States Air Forces Europe (USAFE) had disposed of almost 80 percent of engines, 53 percent of technical supplies, 43 percent of vehicles and 40 percent of munitions. The road-block on faster decommissioning of equipment and ammunition was due to the Surplus Property Act of October 1944 and the legislative procedures required for that. To speed up the processes involved, on 18 September 1945 it was replaced by the Surplus Property Administration, moving it from the Treasury Department to the Department of Commerce.

The sheer scale of disposing of surplus stock is displayed by the transfers list through bulk sales agreements with the British, French and Italian governments, the first being entered into with the British in March 1946 for a contract figure of $532 million. The sale of aircraft originally costing $120,000 apiece were disposed of at little more than $19,000 and this deficit to the US government raised eyebrows in Congress where the immediate cessation of the Lend-Lease agreement was felt to be some small compensation for the bargain-basement price paid by allies for materiel redundant to US use. By January 1947 the Air Materiel Command (AMC) declared $4.8 billion in surplus property broken down into a variety of war assets or awaiting salvage.

The quantity of material retained was however, a testament to production levels higher than anything achieved by any country since the start of the industrial revolution. On 1 May 1946 there were 24,114 aircraft in the United States of which 15,050 were placed in storage or issued to reserve organisations. This inspired

The Bell Aircraft assembly line for its P-39 fighter epitomises the intense industrial mobilisation of national resources as a result of fighting both Germany and Japan during the Second World War, a capacity which would provide unprecedented supply chains during the Cold War. (Bell Aircraft)

development of a new environmental preservation process involving a layer of webbing applied over each airframe on which was sprayed a liquid that hardened into a protective envelope. That process never did provide the total solution and several new materials and processes ensued to make it effective. The balance was divided into 8,224 preserved airframes and 840 declared excess to requirements.

At the end of the war a freeze had been imposed on modifications and planned upgrades to operational aircraft types until it could be determined whether they would be required in future. General Arnold said that he did not want to 'shoe any more dead horses'! Materiel Command experienced a reduction in personnel, falling from 25,443 in July 1945 to 8,308 by 1 January 1946, further reductions lowering that to 2,871 by the end of that year. With numbers of men and materiel in decline, units and stations were restructured, wound up, reduced or changed completely, a track of these being almost impossible to maintain except on a daily basis as orders were received, sometimes superseded and at other times countermanded higher up the chain.

In March 1946 the AAF had 47,544 personnel in the European theatre and 2,555 in the Mediterranean theatre with headquarters for Europe in Wiesbaden, West Germany, from September the previous year. To this command was assigned the XII Tactical Air Command with two fighter wings, a reconnaissance group and one photo-reconnaissance group together with auxiliary units. At this date the AAF supported 71,959 personnel in the Pacific supporting the Eighth and Twentieth Air Forces comprising the Far East Air Forces and the Fifth, Seventh and Thirteenth Air Forces. These boasted six very-heavy-bombardment (VHB) groups with B-29s, nine fighter groups, two light-bombardment (LB) groups and a disparate range of two troop-carrier, three tactical reconnaissance, five air-sea rescue, five night-fighter, two liaison, two tow-target and two very-long-range photographic reconnaissance squadrons.

In other theatres the rundown was even more severe. By March 1946 China had only 7,668 AAF personnel in country, a small fraction of the total previously operating there. The air phase of the Burma campaign was concluded when Rangoon came back into Allied hands. Known as Eastern Air Command, it had been disbanded in June 1945. The need for logistical support fell away markedly and from a peak of 313,868 personnel in August 1945, Air Transport Command (ATC) was reduced to 59,680 by December 1946. There was a significant increase in mission role when it took over the Army Airways Communications System (AACS), the AAF Weather Service, the Aeronautical Chart Service, the Flying Safety Service and the Air Sea Rescue Service. But the ATC was given a unique role in June 1946 when it became responsible for liaison with civil airline operators and for supply information to the AMC.

Fighting the War

We will deal with this in much greater detail when examining the state of the aircraft industry in the period 1945–1949 but for purposes of comparison the total wartime production by type is highly relevant and essential to place the post-war period in context. As measured by factory acceptances from US and Canadian factories building under licence, in 1940 the Army took on 6,028 aircraft of which 1,194 were light, medium or heavy bombers and 1,689 were fighters, the remainder being reconnaissance, transport and trainer types. That increased to 19,445 acceptances in 1941 and to 47,685 in 1942, the number of fighter types falling from 28 percent of all acceptances in 1940 to 22 percent in 1942.

Only in 1942 had the AAF entered the war with combat operations in Europe and the demands of that theatre would materially affect the balance between roles. Total acceptances of all types increased to 85,433 aircraft in 1943, to 95,272 in 1944 and 46,865 in 1945. In those three years, however, fighters accounted for 28 percent, 41 percent and 46 percent of delivered airframes respectively. The reasons for this are clear: the need for long-range fighter escort was evident by 1943 and essential from 1944 so production increased to fill that requirement with P-51 and P-47 variants; and the urgent need to sweep the *Luftwaffe* from the skies over occupied Europe to allow free passage for bomber formations and the D-Day landings of June 1944.

Dissection of bomber acceptance figures which will be found in Volume 2 of this series will show how the strategic requirements affected the division of types into light, medium, heavy and very heavy bombers, the latter being a newly generated category to accommodate the B-29. But the production of fighters was linked to that of the bombers because of the need to provide sufficient fighters for escort and for achieving air superiority, which was generally, although not completely, achieved by the time of the D-Day landings in June 1944. This had been particularly important to gain control over the skies to minimise enemy air attacks on the invasion fleet and on-shore forces.

Of the three dominant fighter types of the war, Curtiss delivered 13,738 P-40s, North American Aviation produced 14,686 P-51s and Republic Aviation provided 15,683 P-47 variants. Overall, the AAF accepted 69,048 fighters during the 1940–1945 period, 29.79 percent of the total 231,748 aircraft of all types. In addition to these deliveries for AAF use, additional production quotas were manufactured for the US Navy and to supply British, Russian and Chinese allied air forces. When these are included the total number of fighters produced increases to 101,714 of all types.

Notwithstanding the acceptances from industry, the total number of AAF aircraft on strength declined from a peak of 78,757 in June 1944 to 69,089 at VE Day, 59,641 on VJ Day and 30,035 by the end of 1946. Of the total aircraft on hand, losses were 79,036 for the period when America declared war in December 1941 to the end of 1946, peak losses being 32,933 (41.6 percent of all in this period), which occurred in 1944 when 11,995 were lost. That represents a loss rate of 400 each day. As related above, increasing numbers of aircraft of all types were held in storage, the number of fighters with AMC holding above 4,000 all the way from November 1945 with only a small reduction to 3,930 by the end of 1946.

Reorganisation

By July 1946 the strength of the AAF had declined from 213 groups to just 52, of which only two were anywhere near full strength in equipment and manpower. From a paper strength of 2,411,294 in March 1944 the number of personnel was down to 450,626 by July 1946. In the preceding 12 months alone, the AAF had lost more than 1.8 million personnel. The low point would be reached in May 1947 when the AAF had 303,614 personnel. Moreover, from a wartime peak of 388,295 pilots in May 1945, by July 1946 the AAF had only 72,983 left in the service.

The early implementation of a demobilisation programme locked in a sequence of procedures to reduce government defence budgets and to cut down unnecessary equipment and manpower levels. At peak the US had spent 41 percent of Gross Domestic Product (GDP) on defence, twice that spent during the First World War, which was itself twice that apportioned for the American Civil War of 1861–1865. In 1945 the US federal government was spending $82.9 billion of its $92.7 billion budget on the war, a staggering 89 percent. Neither was there an installed foreign policy plan for what would be required, either

A recruiting poster from the Second World War embedded a message of national commitment and a unified approach to national defence which would resonate throughout the geopolitical post-war challenges. (USAAF)

in expenditure, men or materiel for the post-war world. As noted in a subsequent section, factors related to manufacturing and production would determine what was affordable for the AAF.

Whereas expenditure during the Second World War had supported urgent requirements for increased production and firepower, post-war requirements would be shaped more by the work which was to be done by the air forces and by the capabilities afforded through the new technologies. These were increasingly rewriting the way the defence of the United States could be expedited and on what the peacetime country could afford. As will be shown in Volume 2, the atom bomb reshaped the old imperative and influenced foreign policy, the nature of war and the very definition of offence, defence and the new-found and increasingly dominant concept of deterrence. These factors would drive requirements in both fighters and bombers.

The growing estrangement between the United States and the Soviet Union bore heavy on the rapidly evolving foreign policy initiatives of the American government and a summary background helps an understanding of why some decisions were made and for the reasons they were. During 1945 few could have predicted how quickly relations between allies would change. Negative messages were coming back from Moscow regarding Soviet intentions over its obligations agreed at key conferences. The Yalta conference of 4–11 February 1945 convened between the United States, Britain and the Soviet Union guaranteed freedoms of self-determination for the liberated countries of Europe. But there were uncertainties in the commitments.

Manpower shortages pushed ethnic minorities into manufacturing with special education programmes putting racial minorities into higher learning for skilled jobs. (NARA)

At the Potsdam Conference of 17 July to 2 August 1945 the demarcation lines between Soviet and non-Soviet zones of occupation were decided but the leadership had changed: President Franklin D Roosevelt had died and President Harry S Truman replaced him at the conference table while Prime Minister Winston Churchill was in the process of being replaced through the ballot box by Clement Attlee. Roosevelt had trusted Stalin and saw an ally in which there could be strong relations between their two countries. Churchill distrusted Stalin and nurtured in secret his support for a possible pre-emptive strike on Russia, until close advisers and military officials in London buried that as being neither plausible nor desirable. Truman had misgivings about Stalin but was focused on rebuilding a peace economy in the United States.

George F Kennan returned from his role at the US Embassy in Moscow with grave foreboding about Soviet intentions and Navy Secretary James V Forrestal warned of a potential clash with the Union of Soviet Socialist Republics. Kennan wrote an 8,000-word telegram to the State Department in response to a request from Washington DC. In that, Kennan advocated 'containment' of the Soviet Union and the setting up of a 'ring of steel' to isolate the totalitarian regime, a precursor to Churchill's 'iron curtain'. Tensions were raised further in March 1946 when Stalin refused to withdraw his troops from Iran and in August two US transport aircraft were shot down while flying over Yugoslavia, already considered little more than a puppet of Moscow.

As the Kennan telegram circulated, and was published anonymously in the influential journal *Foreign Affairs*, concerns that would impact US defence planning began to influence policy, hardening Truman's stance on Moscow. It would have little impact on either tactical or strategic defence postures until the Korean War of 1950–1953 when the situation changed dramatically and in a positive direction for certainty in both defensive and offensive planning. From the Korean War the ideologue of 'containment' would dominate air policy for the next decade or so.

Integration of bombers, fighters, reconnaissance types, transport and liaison aircraft were the received complement in the combat commands. In this way the structure was completely different to, for instance, the Royal Air Force where since 1936 there had been separate operational duties assigned to different commands within the organisational structure. Fighters were the role type for RAF Fighter Command and bombers for RAF Bomber Command. The origin and evolution of the AAF had dedicated air forces for regional

Freshly minted Republic P-47N Thunderbolt fighters in formation for a photoshoot, a type used effectively by the AAF in all theatres and the mainstay of late-war attack and fighter-bomber roles. (USAAF)

theatres and zones of responsibility but with a mix of fighters and bombers for carrying out their duties.

Numbered air forces evolved within the Army Air Corps, which was so renamed from its original identity as the Army Air Service (AAS) on 2 July 1926, and were established on 19 October 1940 primarily for the defence of the United States. The AAS became the AAF on 20 June 1941. The five numbered aviation districts covered the continental United States and were known by Arabic numerals, changing to written words, for instance the 5th Air Force to the Fifth Air Force from 18 September 1941. As a general rule, these conventions relaxed after the war, although numbered air forces were generally assigned to tactical units. Researchers will note that in scrutinising unit reports, these conventions are frequently seen to have been ignored and a mix of Arabic and Roman figures are observed.

The first major plan for the organisation of the post-war AAF was put into effect on 21 March 1946 with the establishment of three combat commands: Strategic Air Command (SAC), Tactical Air Command (TAC) and Air Defense Command (ADC). In addition there was Air Materiel Command (AMC), Air Training Command (ATC), Air Transport Command (ATC), Air Proving Ground and Air University Command. The Continental Air Force was disbanded and became headquarters for SAC while the newly independent US Air Force (USAF) would get Air Research & Development Command (ARDC), Continental Air Command (ConAC) from 1948 to 1968, and the jointly run Military Air Transport Service (MATS), from 1948 to 1966. ConAC was primarily responsible for the Air National Guard and the Air Force Reserve until deactivated in 1968 and replaced by Headquarters, Air Force Reserve (AFRES).

Containment

Under the Army and the Navy, the AAF had no congressionally mandated charter for its organisation and composition. The intention to separate the AAF from the Army had been established in 1943 and the long and fascinating story as to how that came about is not for these pages. Suffice to say that long before the end of the war the AAF was reconfiguring and planning how that would occur and under what credentials it would become the first independent Air Force for the United States. The total restructuring of the US military is also a story to be told elsewhere but it would involve the establishment of the Department of Defense (DoD), managed from the Pentagon in Washington DC embracing the Air Force, Army, Navy and Marine Corps.

Enunciation of what would become known as the Truman Doctrine on 12 March 1947 was the first political edict that served as a standard for defence policy, both at home and in foreign lands. As written, it defined the purpose of US foreign policy as being one in which American support would be provided to democracies threatened by totalitarian powers and specifically identified the Soviet Union as the greatest threat. It responded to the urging of 'containment' espoused by Kennan and Forrestal and would greatly influence the direction of resources and budget requests at the Department of Defense and would lead directly to the formation of the North Atlantic Treaty Organization on 4 April 1949.

As a category of combat aircraft, fighters would be deployed for various roles in all three combat commands and a summary description of each displays the variety of functional responsibilities the post-war fighter held in the USAF. Most important to the operational evolution and deployment of fighters was TAC and ADC, with SAC taking fighters for bomber protection and for the defence of foreign bases as well as support for reconnaissance activity and for escorting mid-air refuelling operations.

When TAC was formed on 21 March 1946 it was based at Tampa, Florida but two months later it moved to Langley Field, Virginia with the Third, Ninth and Twelfth Air Forces, although the Third was inactivated on the 1 November. The stated objective of the TAC was:

to participate in joint operations with ground and/or sea forces; to co-operate with the Air Defense Command in the air defense mission; to operate independently in offensive operations; to train units and personnel for the maintenance of the tactical forces in all parts of the world; to co-operate with Army Ground Forces in training of airborne troops; to perform such special missions as the Commanding General, Army Air Forces may direct.

A Republic P-47N of the 128th Fighter Squadron, 116th Fighter Group of the Georgia Air National Guard seen at Marietta in 1946. (USANG)

To carry out its mission, ADC planned to use six air forces, one for each Army Area. The First Air Force would be responsible for the New York-New England territory. The Eleventh Air Force, reactivated at Olmsted Field, Pennsylvania, on 13 June 1946, would have the region of which the corners are Indiana, Pennsylvania, Virginia, and Kentucky. The Fourteenth Air Force, reactivated at Orlando Army Air Base, Florida, on 24 May 1946 would be assigned the south-eastern states of Tennessee, Mississippi, Alabama, North and South Carolina, Georgia, and Florida. The Tenth, reactivated at Brooks Field, on 24 May 1946, would have jurisdiction over New Mexico, Texas, Oklahoma, Arkansas, and Louisiana. The Second Air Force, activated at Fort Crook, Nebraska, on 6 June 1946, would serve Wyoming, Colorado, North and South Dakota, Nebraska, Kansas, Minnesota, Iowa, Missouri, Wisconsin, Illinois, and Michigan. The Fourth Air Force, at Hamilton Field, California, would defend the eight westernmost states.

Key to a restructuring and reorganisation of the AAF was the realisation that future wars would not have the luxury of time for preparation and mobilisation. When General Arnold handed over command of the AAF on 15 February 1946 to General Carl Spaatz he forwarded a requirement from the Air Staff for an Air Force capable of supporting operations at short notice anywhere around the world. They set the requirement for a peacetime Air Force of 70 groups and 22 specialised squadrons together with an adequate air transport force. To some extent this ran counter to the intricate and detailed plans for demobilisation which had been planned since 1943–1944 but the realities of what would soon be called the Cold War required a very different Air Force to the one that played such a vital role in the Second World War.

It was this requirement that pushed the Command structure of 21 March 1946 and it did ensure the most efficient way of removing old designs and redundant technology in aircraft designs now rapidly overtaken by the jet age and the influx of electronics and radar. But it was the Air Staff requirement for 70 groups that set the global strategic bombing force as key to fighting and winning future wars. It was with this mandate and the aforementioned restructuring that the United States Air Force was established on 18 September 1947 with Forrestal named the first Secretary of Defense and W Stuart Symington Secretary of the Air Force.

It was Symington's fate to confront Forrestal over the pledged 70-group Air Force when he fought against attempts to substantially reduce that to a much lower level. Symington brought a determination to fight hard to keep the Air Force strong while the political leadership sought to reduce the armed services by cutting the budget and stopping advanced technology projects, suspiciously regarded by many politicians as a means of extracting more funding from the government. His message had purpose as he became one of the first voices to warn against complacency over the rising influence of communism in Russia and China, proclaiming the need for 'massive retaliation' in the event of war with the Soviet bloc.

Symington had skill in crafting budget-saving methods to achieve the same objectives with less money, a capability which would prove crucial in the years ahead when the Truman administration attempted a 'dollar blockade' on Air Force funding. In his own words, 'Management Control Through Cost Control'. Symington would remain in post until 24 April 1950 when he became chairman of the National Securities Board, becoming a Senator in 1955 from which position he devoted much time and attention in Congress to the needs of the Air Force.

General Carl Spaatz, the first United States Air Force Chief of Staff, took up the post on 26 September 1947. He had 33 years of service experience, 32 years as a pilot and had been commanding general of the Army Air Forces for 18 months. Spaatz had the unique experience of commanding the US strategic air campaign in Europe and then against Imperial Japan when the war over Europe ended. Spaatz supported a strong, strategic air force and campaigned for a strong tactical air arm and the operational integration with land and sea forces in the event of war.

Two North American P-51H Mustang fighters which would be replaced by a new generation of jet-powered interceptors. The second aircraft (44-6315) was destroyed in a flying accident in August 1946 when it went out of control while 'escorting' a B-29 for an air show. (USAF)

Spaatz used his experience of the Air Corps and the Army Air Forces to warn that in a future war there would be no time for mobilisation, as had been necessary after the attack on Pearl Harbor on 7 December 1941. He wanted an air force capable of achieving through a voluntary recruitment programme a capability ready to fight at immediate notification. Spaatz found it irksome that the only constraint on that was the short-term approach taken by the Truman administration to run down the armed services and cut budgets. In that, he had many friends in the Air Force hierarchy. It became a tiring struggle and he resigned in April 1948.

On 30 April 1948, General Hoyt S Vandenberg succeeded Spaatz and carried the same message to his political masters, advocating a strong and resilient fighting force capable of instant response to an unprovoked attack. To some, he was just doing his job and he was accused of that by detractors in Congress. The message convinced several Congressional leaders, however, and the fight with the White House reached a new and febrile level when President Truman refused to sign the 1949 defence budget and release funds for the Air Force voted on by Congress. The matter was complex and in defence of Truman's budget-cutting programme, his administration reduced government outlays from $92.7 billion in 1945 to $42.6 billion in 1950, reducing the deficit from 103.9 percent of GDP to 78.6 percent. However, in achieving that fiscally prudent goal, he had reduced overall defence spending from 38 percent of GDP to 4.6 percent in the same period.

While the structure of the nascent USAF remained in force, with independence came a certainty that SAC was the most important of the three combat commands as this was responsible for carrying the atomic bomb to targets, presumed to be the Soviet Union, and that this defined the priority given to building that force to a high level. It also inexorably resulted in the concept of 'massive retaliation' on the basis that there would be no graduated response to attack in any sector controlled by the United States and that a full retaliatory strike was a consequence of no debate. So it was that fighters would be a crucial element in that each of the three combat commands required such aircraft to fulfil their respective roles and responsibilities. The progress in building a credible strategic bombing force will be covered in Volume 2.

The Political Backdrop

To set events in context and to place the relative positions of the political establishment and the military in balance, the changing foreign and defence policy of the United States is highly relevant to the story of American air power in the period of peace between the end of the Second World War, officially in September 1945, and the beginning of the Korean War in June 1950. This volume covers the period from 1945 to 1949 and brings the story up to the formation of the North Atlantic Treaty Organization (NATO) but in that time great changes were made to the way the Truman administration sculpted foreign policy and crafted its defence budget. Pivotal to both was the urgent requirement for getting the economy back on a peacetime footing and establishing a balanced budget. Over the four-year period much would change to influence that.

The post-war world would be largely defined by the proceedings of the Potsdam Conference of July-August 1945 at which were set the conditions for political borders and partitioning of East and West Europe, aspects which would shape US air policy for the next 45 years. (NARA)

The international backdrop to events in this period begins with the establishment of the United Nations (UN) in which 50 countries met in San Francisco on 25 April 1945 and began to write the UN Charter which was adopted on 25 June and in effect from 24 October. Concern to support independent Greece and Turkey was the first step toward a more interventionist policy for the United States, although this would only marginally influence military deployments overseas. On 21 February 1947 the British government informed the United States that it could no longer afford to provide economic assistance to those two countries and on 12 March the Truman administration pledged $400 million in aid to stem the encroaching threat of communism.

It was in announcing this that the Undersecretary of State Dean Acheson coined the phrase 'domino theory' when proposing that, unless the victorious nations rose up and defended the rights of free people everywhere, democracy would be overthrown by violent means perpetrated by communist insurgents and fellow travellers supporting extreme and autocratic ideologies. The financial support for Greece and Turkey would also set conditions for the Marshall Plan, announced on 3 April 1948, and provide economic assistance to the democratic countries of Western Europe. In turn, that would establish a favourable condition for NATO, formally established on 4 April 1949.

Almost without intent, and armed with the purposeful prose of Dean Acheson invoking a police-action to contain communism, the United States inherited responsibility around the world for countries and states abandoned by allies on the verge of bankruptcy. Determined to quell the seemingly expanding tide of pro-communist states, the task of containing communism fell to the US military and on the national foreign policy. This had a significant effect on the way US defence requirements evolved throughout this four-year period and the needs of the USAF increased. With expanded defence needs came increased reliance on fighter forces.

With Greece and Turkey already dependent on US aid, in February 1947 the British declared that it was unwilling to retain its mandate in Palestine and handed over responsibility to the United Nations. But the UN had no military force *per-se* and the interest of the United States grew as it alone would be sought to control revolts and internecine conflict that could threaten a vacuum which Stalin would seek to fill. At the UN, Britain abstained from participating in the partition plan for Palestine, walked away from its involvement going back to the Balfour Declaration of 2 November 1917 and tipped the area into a confrontation between Jews and Arabs. The ripple-effect added new responsibilities to US foreign policy with direct effect on the need for armed forces.

Each event was a landmark shift in the initial policy of the United States immediately after the Second World War and would greatly influence decisions made regarding military preparedness, the level of funding required and the way the Air Force planned its structure, procurement and deployment decisions. The immediate aftermath of the war saw policies close to those of the Roosevelt administration, which came to an end with the death of Franklin D Roosevelt on 12 April 1945. Roosevelt had trusted Stalin and worked to construct a post-war Europe favouring the free and democratic choices of liberated nations, trusting the Soviet leader to allow open elections.

By 1946 it was clear that this would not happen and Truman became increasingly alarmed at the Russian grip on Eastern European countries occupied by Soviet forces. The priority given to demobilisation was seen by an increasing majority of American politicians as a mistake, recognising that Stalin was gripped with a paranoia assuaged only by the use of these buffer states as corridors which he could use to defend against in any attack from the West.

General Hoyt Vandenberg rallied support for fighter forces when confronting the Truman administration's drive to reduce the defence budget in an overall push to cut government funding. (NARA)

The US State Department began to take an increasingly hard line as evidence of Soviet duplicity built up, the Potsdam agreement of 1 August 1945 which appeared to endorse self-determination for countries formerly occupied by Germany during the Second World War being disregarded by Moscow.

Specific policy transitions toward an all-out Cold War resulted from Soviet intransigence, Russian belligerence and a renewal of assertions from the Truman administration aimed at reassuring West European democracies and warning potential aggressors against pre-emptive military action. As noted earlier, they were enshrined within the Truman Doctrine of 12 March 1947 which provided US support for democratic countries against authoritarian threats. Through this, unsaid and undocumented were efforts to mobilise a more engaged clandestine surveillance of Soviet territories and to use Air Force reconnaissance capabilities to maintain knowledge about Russian military deployment and currency with Soviet capabilities.

The potential danger in confronting Soviet ambitions was demonstrated by the Berlin blockade of 24 June 1948 to 12 May 1949, whereby rail, road and canal access to West Berlin was stopped as those routes passed through Soviet-occupied eastern Germany to the divided former capital. These events had great influence in reversing a post-war decline in defence expenditure. In absolute terms, the US defence budget fell from $111.9 billion in fiscal year 1945 to $58.2 billion in 1946, to $15.5 billion in 1947 and $11 billion in 1948. Responding to the worsening international situation, the defence budget for 1949 increased to $14.8 billion with a further increase to $15.5 billion in 1950.

It is against this backdrop that the ebb and flow of fighter development moved across those four years between 1945 and 1949, with the deteriorating international situation fuelling a determination to rebuild the Air Force with a new generation of equipment. There were many technical advancements introduced from material found in German factories and from a renewal of research and development in the United States. In several respects the post-war period began with a greater level of uncertainty than had been anticipated and the challenge was to keep alive the opportunity for exploiting the jet engine, new wing designs and the possibility of supersonic flight.

2
BUILDING FOR WAR

During the Second World War the US aviation industry had achieved high standards in technical development while securing unprecedented production levels. The challenges had been enormous, as new engineering processes and high manufacturing standards were required to produce safe and reliable aircraft, each design demonstrating optimum survivability and the highest achievable performance levels. Clearly, for the peacetime/deterrent-orientated Air Force, costs would be an important parameter in procurement cycles. Although a lot of airframes had been scrapped, sold or placed in a mothball state, the new generation of jet aircraft would require new models on a frequent basis. Especially as the technology was rapidly evolving and what was acceptable one year could be out of date in the following year.

Fighter production prices quoted to the government usually ran to the 150-index measure, for a production run of 300 aircraft. In other words, the median cost value plus a fixed profit margin. As a rule, as the number of aircraft produced double the cost falls to 80 percent of the initial value. In industry, this was known as the 'eighty percent curve'. For evaluating costs to set the price, industry standards at the end of the war adopted a level of five labour-hours per pound of structural work, which at the time was $15 for fighters and $10 for transport types. The higher labour cost for fighters was due to the smaller space within which to work, necessitating additional work-hours, and a requirement for a wider and more complex range of fittings.

Specific costs were defined by several factors, one of which was the type of material selected and here too accessibility was a factor. Low-drag wings on fighters were also more labour-intensive due to the slender size and restricted work-space reducing the number of people working on a specific section in a given time. It also increased the structural weight due to a reduction in the cross-section inertia level requiring more material to carry the bending loads. The increasing use of 75ST aluminium in place of 24ST metal increased production costs due to new tooling required for dimpling and bending, the characteristics of which were completely different. Adapting to a new material was one of the most costly factors in higher prices.

Nevertheless, headquartered in Pittsburgh, Pennsylvania, the Aluminum Company of America (ALCOA) provided 75S in large volume for aircraft construction. This product contains 90 percent aluminium with magnesium, zinc and copper as its major alloying constituents and was produced commercially as Alclad sheet and extruded shapes. Tensile strength of the fully heat-treated 75ST was about 88,000psi (604,120kPa). In sheet form it had a strength of 77,000psi (530,915kPa) while the yield strength of extruded sheets was about 67,000psi (461,965kPa), around 50 percent higher than that for 24ST. The new material was used widely for wing spars, with sheet and extrusions used for wing and fuselage structures.

The new jet engines offered greater performance as they were able to power fixed-wing aircraft to greater speeds because they were not restricted by the loss of efficiency with propellers above about 450mph (727kph). They

Architect of US foreign policy and author of the 'containment' policy and the fear of a 'domino-effect' over communist takeover among disenfranchised countries, Dean Acheson is sworn in as Secretary of State by Chief Justice Fred Vinson on 21 January 1949. (NARA)

were able to use a kerosene-based fuel, cheaper than the leaded 100-octane gasoline used in the later, double-row piston engines. Moreover, jet engines were simpler to maintain than reciprocating engines. They were able to operate at greater efficiency at higher altitude but early engines were prodigious consumers of fuel and gave airframes a much shorter range on a specific range/fuel ratio. They also introduced problems with cooling. Invariably buried within fuselage or wings, the additional heat produced by the jet required special solutions to prevent excess thermal soak-back into the structure.

A considerable challenge was in the shift from primarily piston-powered to jet fighters, with overlap between types requiring training and conversion programmes to provide engineers and technicians with the necessary information. There was also a major problem with rushing into operational service aircraft types which had great growth potential in terms of performance and capability. While operating units sought types with legacy potential through subsequent variants, ensuing continuity of familiarity for pilots and technicians and commonality of support equipment and servicing infrastructure, manufacturing and manpower commitments could become excessive.

One example of this was a fighter widely employed in Europe and the Pacific which required expenditure of 35,000 engineering man-hours up to the prototype stage but about 1.855 million man-hours for improvements and modifications. It is largely because of this ratio, which was not at all uncommon for single-seat and two-seat fighters of the period, that it was usually more cost effective to develop competitive prototypes than rush forward with a single-source selection of an un-competed design.

As an example of how new technology tilts the ratio of integration costs, when North American Aviation decided to incorporate the laminar-flow wing into the P-51D, from research conducted by the government National Advisory Committee for Aeronautics (NACA), it took 40,000 man-hours to integrate the new design on the assembly line, accounting for 15 percent of all development man-hours on this aircraft. As the requirements for fighters grew almost exponentially and the technical possibilities increased at an almost parallel rate, the direct engineering man-hours flipped in favour of bombers between 1940 and 1945. In 1940 an average bomber required 329,415 man-hours compared with 131,562 for a fighter. By 1945, as fighters became more complex, these figures had switched to 200,321 and 775,574, respectively.

In testimony to the Senate Military Affairs Committee in 1945, R E Gillmor, vice-president of the Sperry Corporation speaking on behalf of the Aircraft Industries Association, said that:

> There is a widespread impression that the chief effort and greatest cost in developing aircraft occur during the initial stages of product research leading to and including the design and construction of the first model usually called the

One of the more successful twin-engine night fighters, the Northrop P-61 was developed in cooperation with the British and remained in front-line service until 1950. Although only 706 were built it went through a large number of variants, upgrades and modifications. (USAF)

prototype…One of our companies spent a total of $1,777,311 and 526,000 engineering man-hours to bring a fighter plane through the wind tunnel and prototype stages. But it expended more than three times this amount in money and man-hours for production engineering to develop this model and incorporate improvements to meet maximum performance requirements.

He went on to cite numerous examples to verify this.

Industrial Adjustments

Against the head-winds of a rapidly advancing level of technology both in materials and engines came the industry shrinkage due to cancelled orders and the reconfigured production lines moving from combat types to commercial aircraft. For a time, a surfeit of wartime transport types would form the backbone of a new surge in passenger travel but industry would quickly come to accept new standards with priority on reliability, comfort, safety and efficiency. An industry that had grown to be the world's largest single manufacturing producer was called upon to make seismic changes to its product range for a very different market, one in which competition was uppermost and the needs of the market, although expanding, more constrained than had been the case for more than five years when aircraft for the military had dominated development and production.

Retraction in the industry was rapid, however. From a peak of producing almost 100,000 aircraft in 1944, by the end of 1945 three separate reduction phases cancelled orders for 75,700 aircraft at a saving to the government of $13 billion. That caused a reduction of around a million employees to leave a scant 150,000 on pay cheques. Companies were affected in different ways and at various levels according to their specialities and potential for new orders. There was still work to be done bringing in jet replacements for propeller-driven fighters and with an emphasis on strategic bombing as the core function of the post-war air forces companies such as Boeing had plenty of development work in hand to see them through. Fighter manufacturers had decidedly mixed fortunes, as identified through their war record and immediate post-war prospects, projects and programmes.

During the war, Bell Aircraft Corporation had produced 7,229 P-39 Airacobra and P-63 Kingcobra fighters for delivery to the Soviet Union, of which 5,180 had been moved by air all the way, while supplying a further 5,662 to the US and Allied air forces. Bell had also produced 663 B-29s at its Marietta, Georgia, facility at an average rate 50 percent higher than predicted at the outset. Along with P-39 and P-63 production, B-29 work stopped at the end of the war, although Bell had a 100 percent success record on B-29s delivered, all of which were tested by Bell crews, flight tested by the AAF and delivered by ferry pilots without a single failure or loss. Post-war, Bell retained work on the RP-63, a specially armoured variant of the Kingcobra with almost a ton of armour plate treated so as to cause an impacting bullet to disintegrate on impact.

Design and production demands on North American Aviation had increased rapidly during the war years with its Inglewood facility managing three programmes of its own design, the AT-6 Texan trainer, the B-25 Mitchell and the P-51 fighter. Dallas was producing the AT-6F trainer, the SNJ and the P-51D, with the B-25H and J and the PBJ-1 coming out of Kansas City and the P-51H emerging from the NAA factory alongside the Los Angeles Municipal Airport. In addition, NAA had the P-82 Twin Mustang on test following its first flight on 15 June 1945 and was gearing up for production of the Lockheed P-80 at the Kansas plant. The NAA order was cancelled on 16 May 1945 after tooling was 80 percent finished and the first aircraft was 78 percent complete. The West Coast plant set a national production record in January 1945 for a single type from one plant when it pushed 571 P-51s out the door during that month.

When the war ended, NAA closed operations at the Kansas City and Dallas factories and returned those facilities to the government. Operations focused on completing P-51H production at the West Coast plant in November 1945, replacing it with the P-82 alongside five new and upcoming projects. When the P-51H line closed NAA had completed 15,302 fighters since the national defence programme began in July 1940, representing 14.1 percent of all fighters produced in the United States in that period. It had also produced 15,117 Texan trainers, 25.8 percent of the national total and overall the company had produced 41,203 fighters, trainers and bombers, accounting for 13.6 percent of the total from all US manufacturers. Production had already begun to decline a year before the end of the war with Japan, NAA putting out 24,987 tons of airframe weight in the first six months of 1945 compared with 33,660 tons during the same period in 1944.

Great progress had been made by all US aircraft manufacturers with increasingly efficient use of men and materiel. At NAA's Inglewood factory alone during the 12 months of 1944 there was a 49 percent reduction in man-hours per pound of airframe weight, with a 63 percent reduction at the Kansas City factory and a 64 percent cut at Dallas. P-51s rolled along a conveyor line with an efficiency that Henry Ford could only have imagined, each aircraft fuelled up and the engine subject to a full power run before it rolled out the door, straight to the runway and on to a dispersal airfield. All along the production line, underground tanks for engine oil, coolant and fuel supplied fluids to aircraft rolling along the above-ground production conveyor.

As productivity had increased, employee satisfaction was ensured by a reward scheme for efficiency savings, some 11,301 submissions having been made at NAA alone of which almost 28 percent had been accepted and individuals awarded $82,761 in total through war bonds and stamps. High numbers of women were inducted to the production lines and the first 'demarcation by segregation' plans were put in place when it was realised that women presented a different skill format than men. This established a selection process, assignments on the shop floor being made according to the particular skills required for specific jobs, ensuring a more efficient fit between task and worker.

North American would rapidly transition from reciprocating to reaction engine aircraft and make a major contribution to the emerging generations of fighters, as noted in another chapter. But it also made a major contribution to the industry as a whole and to effective operation of existing aircraft from other manufacturers. With a clear market-lead in training aircraft and concerned at the workload imposed on trainee pilots by a multitude of different cockpit configurations, the company developed a standardised armament control panel. Working closely with the Air Technical Service Command, NAA eliminated errors and confusion and reduced accident and poor score levels caused by a diversity of panel configurations. Especially useful in development of the somewhat radical P-82 Twin Mustang, NAA used one of the largest altitude pressure chambers in the US to begin one of the most extensive engineering and research programmes of any manufacturer.

Northrop delivered the last of its wartime P-61 Black Widow night fighters in January 1946, one of the more outstanding aircraft to arrive in service within a year of the end of the war and to remain in service until 1954. The company had assembled 1,098 aircraft

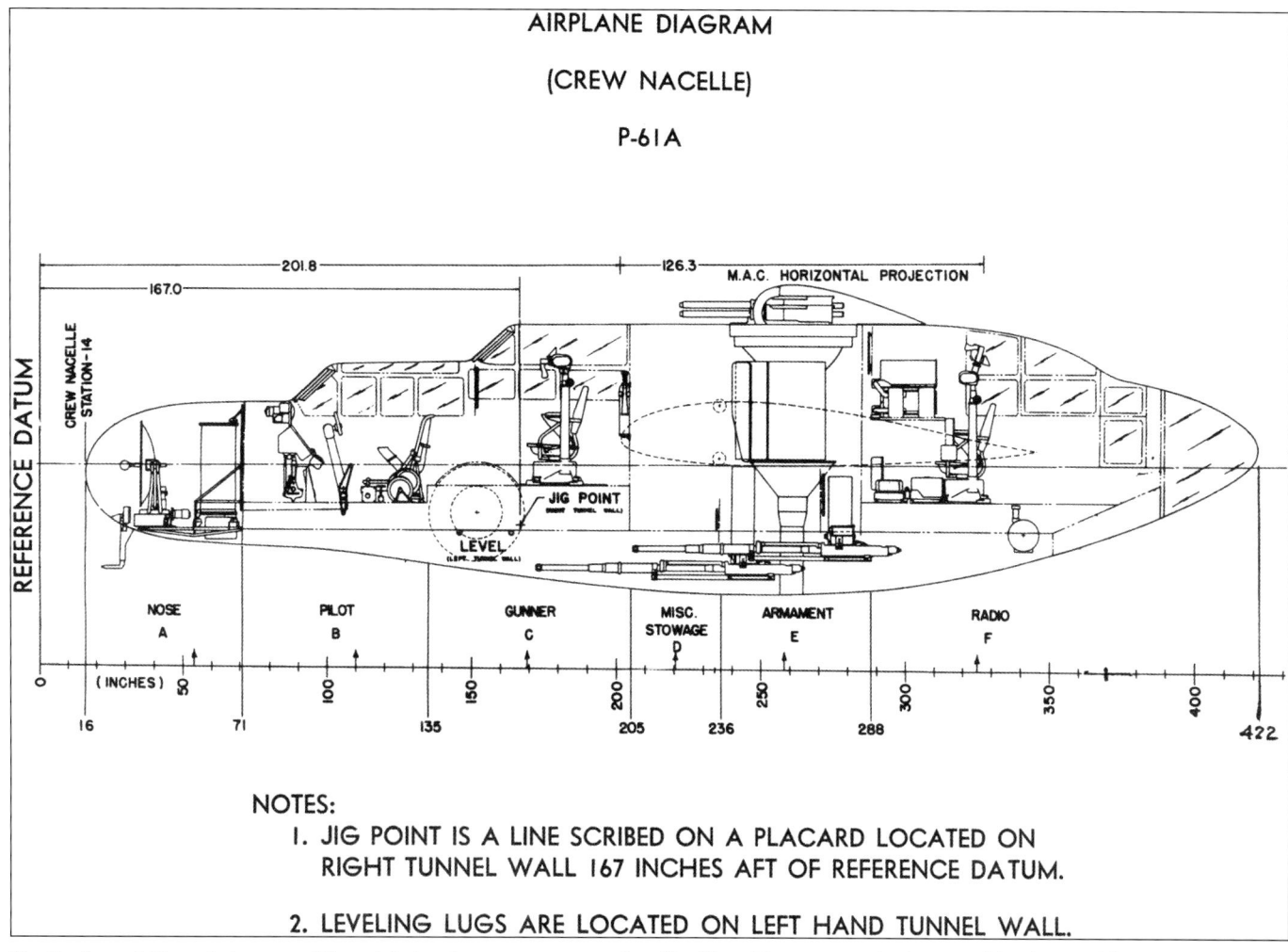

The Northrop P-61 carried a crew of three (pilot, radar operator, gunner) and had four 20mm cannon in the ventral fuselage and four 0.50-calibre machine guns in a remotely operated, fully traversable upper turret. (USAAF)

during the war years in addition to 1,309 tail surface sets, 1,291 nacelles and cowls for PBY5s and 44,832 cowls and 25,068 nacelles for B-17s. Largely a subcontractor, Northrop diversified in prudent attempts to keep its workforce employed and acquired Northrop Gaines, producing industrial wheels and materials handling equipment, and Salisbury Motors manufacturing very small petrol engines, automatic clutches, variable-speed transmissions, scooters and turret trucks.

A significant Northrop engineering development during the war and applicable to post-war applications was the retractable aileron which the company described as follows:

It was designed to incorporate in the Black Widow full-span flaps which made it possible for the plane to land at slow, safe speeds on small landing strips under conditions of extreme low visibility, and to give the Black Widow, which was as big as a medium bomber, an unusual degree of manoeuvrability. The retractable aileron system of the Black Widow was a combination of the conventional type and four 'retractable aileron' panels linked to the aileron control system. These panels worked in unison with the ailerons. The entire system was controlled by the wheel in the cockpit. Roll was induced almost entirely by the retractable ailerons.

Under flight conditions, there was an opening moment on the retractable ailerons. Were it not for the small conventional ailerons which were linked to the retractable ailerons, this opening moment would be translated into a disposition to over-balance. In other words, once the wheel was moved from the neutral position, the retractable aileron would tend to continue its travel out of the wing until fully extended. There was, naturally, a trailing moment on the small conventional aileron.

This trailing moment was just great enough to overcome the opening moment of the retractable ailerons and to impart 'feel' to the system. As the speed of the airplane increased, the opening moment on the retractable ailerons and likewise the trailing moment on the conventional ailerons were increased. The trailing moment on the latter increased at only a slightly greater rate than did the opening moment on the retractable ailerons. As a consequence, control forces did not increase with speed in anywhere near the same proportion as did the forces of ordinary aileron systems.

At high speeds, because of the fact that less force was required, the control could be moved more quickly and, hence, a more rapid rate of roll attained than was possible with the average conventional system under the same circumstances. At slow speeds with the flaps up, the effectiveness of the retractable ailerons was equal to that of the usual system. However, with the flaps down, effectiveness (as expressed in terms of rate of roll with full aileron deflection) was approximately 40 per cent greater than that of the average conventional installation. In addition, the retractable ailerons retained effectiveness down to and past the stall. The ship would roll from side to side in quick response to the wheel. Likewise, the ship could be held straight during a stall with one engine wind milling, while the other was at take-off power.

In addition to the P-61, a derivative of the Black Widow was in development as the F-15 Reporter, a dedicated and unarmed photo-reconnaissance aircraft, and the XB-35 experimental 'flying wing' bomber, which is covered in Volume 2. The F-15 was an all-metal, mid-wing monoplane with a crew of two in a nacelle between the engines and was an exponent of the retractable ailerons which proved that as innovative and effective as they were proclaimed to be and found most optimum application with this type. A total of 36 F-15As were produced and began operations with the Japan Air Material Area at Kisarazu, Japan. The type achieved notable regard for having conducted most of the aerial mapping of North Korea during the war of 1950–1953. Although production was cancelled in 1947, a total of 46 F-15s were built.

One of the main producers of fighter aircraft during the war, and for some time after, Republic Aviation Corporation completed production of the P-47 Thunderbolt in November 1945 with its 15,329th aircraft, development for this class of aircraft continuing with the jet-powered P-84. For a while after the cessation of hostilities, Republic did C-54 reconversion work for American Airlines and in this way was able to retain more of its workforce than would have been possible otherwise. During P-47 production, Republic had built an enormous capacity, operating from 2.7 million ft² (250,830m²) at Farmingdale, New York, and Evansville, Indiana. The Evansville plant was evacuated completely and handed back to the government. But like all manufacturers, Republic suffered from cancelled contracts, cutting its work force from a peak of around 23,000 to about 3,700 after VJ Day, while payrolls for Farmingdale increased to 6,000 employees by March 1946.

Research and Development

Research in the United States for the development of military aircraft began in 1917 on land that incorporated the Huffman Prairie Flying Field, Dayton, Ohio. Supporting expansion and an increase in research work, additional land was acquired in 1924 and named Wright Field in honour of the pioneering work carried out there by the Wright Brothers before the First World War. In July 1931, further expansion took place in an area named Patterson Field, after the aviator Frank Patterson who had been killed in 1918 while flying an experimental DH-4 equipped with a new form of synchronising gear.

Expansion due to war increased the workforce from 3,700 in 1939 to more than 50,000 at both Wright and Patterson, the workload

Key to several engineering developments in the early post-war years, the National Advisory Committee for Aeronautics (NACA) provided a wide range of test facilities and is here represented by a Douglas D-558-II Skyrocket (front), two swept-wing F-86 chase aircraft and a B-29 carrier-plane. (NACA)

moving from a standard working week to rotating shifts for 24/7 operations year-round. Wright Field grew from 40 buildings in 1941 to more than 300 in 1944 and a new modified runway was laid down at Wright Field.

Research quickly focused on new aircraft, more effective weapons and increased efficiency in both categories as production and labour costs became critical to supply cycles at factories and in manufacturing facilities. To facilitate expansion of the manufacturing base, government land and federal installations were turned over to plane-makers and engine-builders in a desperate effort to provide sufficient floor space for production lines. The need for technical improvements driven by operational requirements pushed additional demands on research at Wright and Patterson. When the Air Technical Service Command was formed in August 1944, Wright became subordinate to Patterson but that brought some challenge to morale due to the vertical hierarchy implied.

Not wholly to solve this problem alone, together with adjacent AAF facilities, Patterson and Wright Fields were renamed the Army Air Forces Technical Base on 15 December 1945, the 'Army' being dropped from the name in December 1947. From which date the southern stretch of Patterson Field became Area A, the original Wright Field becoming Area B and the northern portion of Patterson Field becoming Area C where special facilities were installed for testing jet aircraft. Restoration of many activities curtailed by the demands of war included the Army Air Forces Engineering School and the Army Air Forces Institute of Technology. On 13 January 1948 the AAF Technical Base was redesignated the Wright-Patterson Air Force Base.

What the Air Force inherited had been a colossal undertaking, eclipsing anything developed anywhere else in the other belligerent countries. Wright Field was also responsible for supervising a massive procurement effort with frequent visits by up to 700 prime and ancillary manufacturers. In the period of the Second World War, the production cycle was condensed from several years to a few months. Proud of its accomplishments, in October 1945 some 500,000 people visited Wright Field during what was to have been an open-day and due to its popularity was extended to a week, with more than a million people from 26 foreign countries watching both operational and experimental aircraft including static displays of captured German and Japanese aircraft.

By the end of the war there were 14 separate laboratories and five electronics laboratories, of which all except one were at Wright Field. Activity was closely linked to the Muroc Flight Test Base in California and a pilotless aircraft testing centre was set up at Wendover, Utah while facilities at Dover, Delaware, conducted research on rockets for aircraft at the Armament Laboratory. From June 1946 radio research would be conducted at Cambridge Field Station, Massachusetts. Post-war, and following the separation of the Air Force from the Army, extensive inter-service research and development was encouraged by the Pentagon but in reality there was considerable competition for some time, until defined roles and responsibilities were formalised. A not inconsiderable contest arose between the Navy and the Air Force over which service should have responsibility for delivering the strategic nuclear role. That is covered in detail in Volume 2.

The NACA developed the use of electronic computational devices and employed women as 'computers' to carry out complex mathematical calculations for aeronautical engineers and design teams, finding them superior to their male counterparts in this specific type of work. (NACA)

Formed on 27 June 1940, the National Defense Research Committee (NDRC) had primary responsibility for basic research and development but it was disbanded in 1947 when Air Materiel Command took on an increasing amount of this activity, taking over more than 2,000 research projects when the NDRC was disbanded. Post-war at the AMC's Engineering Division the direction of research work shifted from the development of weapons and new aircraft to advanced concepts supporting jet flight and missiles, and from development of specific items of ancillary equipment to integrated systems. There was a concerted effort to use the years of peace to evaluate potentially ground-breaking technologies and to conduct research on advanced concepts. Toward which end there was a concerted push to acquire detailed information on projects underway in German research facilities, with 500 people working to catalogue, index and store 55,000 captured German documents.

The end of the war brought great opportunities for learning from the captured German scientists and engineers themselves who had played major roles in the development of advanced concepts, some of which could have proven useful in the post-war age of jets, high-speed and high-altitude flight. Most were of value for their ideas with innovative and creative engineering. To best utilise these people, immediately after the war the Air Materiel Command supervised the work of 86 senior German engineers and scientists employed at the Wright Field laboratories, and through its Technical Intelligence Department set up in August 1947. These men, employed by the Air Force on 'temporary' contracts included Rudolph Hermann, Walter Lippisch, Heinz Schmitt, Helmut Heinrich, Fritz Doblhoff and Ernst Kugel. Others working directly on rocket projects, principally the notable Wernher von Braun, had gone to the Army at Fort Bliss in Texas.

Of those taken to Wright Field, Hermann had been with the Peenemünde research group working on the V2 and had been in charge of the supersonic wind tunnel at Kochel in the Bavarian Alps. He had worked on possible satellite concepts when such speculative ideas were disapproved of by the German High Command and by the SS which had increasingly taken over the V1 and V2 programmes. At Wright Field, Hermann was assigned to supersonics which were becoming a central part of future fighter design as US manufacturers pushed ahead with high-speed jet aircraft concepts and would begin to outpace government research organisations, including those of the Air Force.

Doblhoff had been working on a helicopter powered by the exhaust from a small jet engine with the efflux channelled through rotor blades which mobilised their rotation through the principle of reaction. His work continued at Wright Field while Lippisch, the noted designer of gliders in the pre-war years brought a wealth of knowledge and experience from funded research at a range of German institutions and experimental facilities. He was head of the Research Institute for Aviation in Vienna, Austria, when the war ended. At Wright Field he worked on the Me 163 rocket-powered interceptor with which he had been associated during the development of this remarkable project.

Supporting that was research at Wright into the Walter HWK-109 rocket motor for the Me 163 and on the chemical combinations for propellants, notably the T-Stoff and C-Stoff which provided an impulse of up to 190lb (86kg) for each pound (0.45kg) of

A Republic F-84F in a wind tunnel at the Ames Aeronautical Laboratory, Moffett Field, California. (NACA)

consumption per second. However, expressed as a consumption rate in lb/hr per pound of thrust, the Walter motor was 13 times greater than that of a conventional jet engine, endurance being sacrificed for sheer speed. With a weight of 365lb (165.5kg) the Walter motor produced a thrust of 3,300lb (14.67kN). There was also interest in the Bachem Ba-349 Natter which used a combination of the HWK-109 liquid propellant rocket motor with four solid propellant Shmidding boosters providing a phenomenal climb rate of 37,000ft (11,277m) per minute. Both Mc 163 and Ba 349 were unlikely contenders for post-war applications and the fundamental technology was of greater interest for other applications.

Dr Heinz Schmitt worked at Wright Field on captured examples of the Jumo 004 turbojet engine which had powered the Me 262, the world's first operational jet fighter to see active service. There was much to learn from the Jumo engine and it provided valuable test experience for turbojets of this type, as there was with other research activity from German institutes and test facilities. In addition to airframes and engines, other German research work provided insight to a broad and increasingly diverse research base for new and innovative technologies.

Supervised by Helmut Heinrich, formerly from the Graf Zeppelin Research Institute, Stuttgart, a small team worked on high-speed ribbon parachutes for retarded bombs, spin-recovery for very light aircraft and as braking 'chutes for jet and rocket-powered aircraft. Considerable development work had been conducted in Germany during the war and the teams at Wright Field worked on tests and concept development, one application of which was to automatically stabilise a tumbling aircraft as the pilot attempted to eject. Ejection seats had also been integrated with this work in Germany but like so many wartime projects in all the belligerent countries, with priority on production and delivery, refinements or low-value research were hard to justify.

Ernst Kugel had been the technical director of the Alfred Schloemann Company in Germany, specialising in rolling mills and hydroelectric presses. He assisted the Air Force in organising detailed drawings of a 30,000 ton hydraulic press built for I G Farben and used for pressed-out propeller blades. This press was five times more powerful than anything in the United States at the time and four other German technicians assisted Kugel with the job of collating the vast quantities of drawings and blueprints in the absence of the actual presses, which could not be brought across from Germany due to their massive size and weight.

All this work involved a lot of German technicians and engineers working with their American contemporaries and tutors and educators were brought in to compile a 75,000-word German-English dictionary of aviation, science and engineering words. Few spoke each other's language and the dictionary was to prove a vital asset for speeding up the dialogue within mixed-nationality teams. The work was headed by Dr Kurt L Leidecker who was on loan from the Behr-Manning Corporation and Rensselaer Polytechnic Institute where he was employed as assistant professor of scientific German. Unique to these Germans was a new form of aeronautical language incorporating completely new terms and phrases to accommodate the new technologies, a 'Nazification of terminology' as the Americans called it.

Working at Wright Field on a voluntary basis as alien employees, the Germans earned between $2.20 and $11 a day, equivalent to approximately £0.55 to £2.75 in 1947. In Britain in 1947 the average wage was £1.05 per day, with technical trades on £1.75. These wages were sent directly to their families or dependents in Germany and in that regard they were hired employees serving abroad (in the United States) as long as their employer, the government, required. In addition, the German workers were paid a further $6 a day for subsistence which they received in cash and this was the same as US civil servants. Accommodation was on a par with that afforded junior officers. Mail was censored and put through the usual official channels but most considered themselves fortunate, compared to living standards in post-war Germany where there were widespread food shortages, disrupted transport and an almost non-existent rail system.

The employment of German workers brought across from Europe at the end of the war had been a hotly contested practice at the US State Department, not least due to the imperative restriction placed upon such people by the Roosevelt administration. Under that stipulation, no 'ardent Nazi' was to be allowed entry into the United States, no matter how valuable they could be to national security. But the technical teams scouring occupied Europe for the fruits of German research work were not going to let that get in the way of securing the services of skilled and professionally competent experts, scientists and engineers capable of providing valued knowledge to the armed services. In an arrangement known as the Paperclip Conspiracy, whereby a paperclip was attached to a request from the military for a work visa, people considered essential to the post-war development of the US armed services were automatically registered as '*not* an ardent Nazi'.

The Bell X-1A rocket-powered transonic/supersonic research aircraft which produced data of value to manufacturers of combat aircraft, although the fighters of the late 1940s were catching up fast with the levels of performance demonstrated by the X-series research types. (NACA)

In truth, a life in the United States secured in this way was a tremendous boost to new opportunities, a secure and well-paid position and a career that only months earlier had seemed shattered and impossible to resurrect. Big names such as the German rocket scientist Wernher von Braun would become icons of a successful transition from autocracy to democracy and in many ways were embraced as exemplars of the American dream, newly converted patriots working for the greater good of a prosperous America. It blended well with the prolific array of air shows, parades and public displays of the US military that exposed Americans who had never left their country during the war to the realities of a Cold War, where a new enemy had erased moral judgements over the last one.

It would be wrong to assume that this influx of new and exotic technology provided, in itself, a major step up for American research and development. Considerable work had been conducted during the last two years of the war to prepare the government and industry for the coming age of jet aircraft, rockets and missiles, of advanced radar systems and increasingly sophisticated electronics. As production of combat aircraft began to decline toward the end of 1944, industry joined the research base to find new ways of staying in business, if not actually increasing their revenues from new government orders for what was colloquially known as R&R – Restoration and Replenishment, the buzz-words for 'business as usual'.

At the end of the war a range of new possibilities was made available through the ancillary industries, many of them being enabling technologies without which new eras in combat aircraft evolution would have been impossible. As jets emerged from aircraft factories and demonstrated their potential at experimental facilities with exceedingly long runways, it was quickly realised that there was a single-point flaw in the plan to push them out for operational duty. Beginning in 1941, the United States Rubber Company of New York began development of new nylon aircraft tyres. As fighters became faster and were landing at higher speed and under increased load, ordinary tyres were incapable of withstanding the stresses involved.

So began a programme that faced greater challenges with the advent of jet fighters. Without the evolved nylon tyre, even the first-generation jets could never have operated from the places to which they were assigned. In combat areas, ruptures decreased from over 15 percent to less than 0.5 percent, strength increasing proportionate to stress resistance to achieve loads never before envisaged and reaching 10 times the load per tyre weight achieved for tyres on road vehicles. New materials were introduced to tyre manufacturing and proved significant in allowing aircraft designers to develop fighters with far higher landing loads and speeds that could have been imagined when the war began. In this and numerous other examples, the ancillary industry enabled the new age of the jet fighter, at least one which could be used operationally and on limited field facilities.

At the top end, with great effort, resources and money Wright Field was working the development of the military aircraft of the present and the future but new capabilities with potential envisaged for the longer term, rested with the NACA. Formed on 13 March 1915 it was to provide research and carry out tests to support the development of US military aviation by bringing together academic research, scientific tests, engineering and government programmes. It had been primarily influenced by the British Advisory Committee for Aeronautics as well as other similar bodies across continental Europe. Late in the day, it was to prove a vital tool for government-funded research on projects and through programmes for which there was no immediate commercial return, to perfect concepts and technology to attract manufacturers to spend their own money on further development, manufacture and production.

With research facilities on aerodynamics at the Langley Aeronautical Laboratory and at the Ames Aeronautical Laboratory from 1939, it gained the Aircraft Engine Research Laboratory at Cleveland Ohio in 1941, known as the Flight Propulsion Research Laboratory from 1947 and as the Lewis Flight Propulsion Laboratory from 1948. Through an expanding range of wind tunnels for general and highly specialised research, and with various test rigs and evaluation facilities together with aircraft on loan from the military, the NACA played a seminal role in advancing the aeronautical sciences, not least through its NACA-series of aerofoil shapes which were utilised internationally by aircraft manufacturers around the world.

In the certain knowledge that the advent of the turbojet engine would usher in a completely new age of high-speed combat aircraft and under pressure from the AAF to develop a research platform, the NACA was deeply involved in development of the X-1 transonic and supersonic research aircraft. But on a theoretical and test basis rather than development of a new aircraft for such a purpose. The NACA assisted the Air Force with development of the X-1, built by Bell Aircraft with two distinctly different aerofoils and thickness ratios and powered by a multi-chamber rocket motor as the performance of existing turbojets was inadequate for transonic flight. Eventually, Bell would produce more X-1s and the NACA would place Bell under contract for the X-2, with which the Air Force had hoped to conduct the first flight through Mach 3.

Piloted by Charles 'Chuck' Yeager on 14 October 1947, the first X-1 exceeded Mach 1 in level flight. However, industry was already catching up and using information

Training and familiarisation became a vital factor in pilot safety on new jet types. Established methods such as the Link trainer helped neophytes on their way to receiving pilot's wings. (NACA)

from German research had already developed the North American F-86. Industry would continue to challenge the NACA with high-speed combat types. The X-1 provided the Air Force with a propaganda tool for proclaiming its unique capabilities after gaining independence from the Army in the previous month. But it was kept from announcing the flight until the trade magazine *Aviation Week* broke the news and burst the security bubble surrounding its achievement.

The NACA had been denied the funds to develop its own research aircraft but, against opposition from the Air Force, in the early 1950s it would eventually obtain approval to place under contract three X-15 aircraft from North American Aviation. These would be used to explore the aerothermal environment during high supersonic and hypersonic flights in a series of 199 air-dropped test runs with only one casualty in that period between 1959 and 1968. In a broader context, the NACA was the only research organisation capable of operating a piloted flying machine in these environments and a lot of that work went on to support development of the National Aeronautics and Space Administration (NASA) Space Shuttle.

The NACA provided an opportunity for engineers to garner data through a new generation of electromechanical calculating machines, as demonstrated here by the Bell Computer at work in the NACA's Ames facility in 1947. (NACA)

Identification

After the AAF became independent and the US Air Force was established on 18 September 1947, it was not long before the wartime type designation system was changed. Based on an alphabetical sequence, on 11 March 1948 the Pursuit (P) types of previous decades became Fighters (F), a group which included a wide range of old and newly redesignated aircraft and new types bridging the transition. Consequently, confusion can be caused by the use of different letters for specific periods and in the following narrative there is necessarily a mix of both P and F prefixes. The only unchanging absolute is the type number as designated by the commissioning authority at the AAF or the USAF and later with the Department of Defense.

A prefix 'X' indicates a prototype (usually more than one) and a 'Y' indicates a pre-production aircraft, deletion of the prefix indicating a full production aircraft type destined for, or in full operational service. Suffix letters applied to the type number indicate a new variant to the same type and an additional number added after a hyphen indicates a Block change on the production line, which usually came in step changes of five as, for example, in P-51D-10, -15, -20, etc. The Block identifiers are rarely used in this book and are relevant only when tracking single or multiple step-changes within a designated type variant. A further set of two letters indicates the subcontractor building that particular aircraft.

Readers will be aware of the serial system used in US military aircraft, whereby the last two numbers of the financial year in which the order was made precede a hyphen followed by the numerical sequence in which the order was approved. This was not necessarily the date on which it was signed but was usually accompanied by a Letter of Intent. In the United States the financial year began on 1 July in the year preceding the numbered year, which was the calendar year beginning on 1 January. For instance, a contract with the designation 43-123 indicates that it was the 123rd aircraft ordered in FY 1943, which would have been in the period between 1 July 1942 and 30 June 1943. When displayed on the tail the serial number was presented in abbreviated form, the first number of the fiscal year together with the suffix hyphen being deleted, so that 43-123 would be displayed as 3123. Moreover, an aircraft with a single-digit serial number of 43-1 would sport a tail number of 3001. Changes did occur in subsequent years and will be noted in subsequent volumes in this series.

Starting in the final years of the Second World War, aircraft were provided with 'buzz' numbers in an attempt to provide a letter and number to readily identify a particular aircraft and prevent pilots 'buzzing' the airfield buildings when returning from a mission. Buzz numbers were a two-letter code identifying the aircraft type with a three-digit number which usually took the last three numbers of the serial. The tradition of applying buzz numbers to the forward fuselage followed a spate of incidents in which the exuberance of returning safely from a combat mission was displayed by way of a dangerous burst of adrenalin vented through a close encounter with the airfield's control tower. It also took on a more serious purpose when spotters in the control tower would read the buzz number to tick off individual aircraft returning safely back to base.

The various colours and marking schemes applied throughout this period are amply covered elsewhere in other sources, both printed and in digital form. With little effort, readers will find a wide range of accessible references detailing the change in national markings and the various finishes applied to fighters of the period, both general and specific. Suffice here to say that the national insignia was displayed on each side of the fuselage aft of the wing and on the lower starboard and upper port wing surfaces with the letters USAF displayed on the opposing wing surfaces.

On occasion, reference will also be made to an MX (Materiel Experimental) programme, the letters standing for Materiel Experimental. Introduced to the Army Air Corp Materiel Division in 1941, the MX classification was raised at Wright Field for identifying

Training moved from initial stages of acceptance for candidate pilots to experience with flying and flying through the Ryan PT-22 Recruit training aircraft. (Julian Herzog)

new research and development programmes for all engineering work and identifying relevant orders, starting with MX-1. The classification embraced a very wide range of defence programmes and was a faster route to obtaining Top Secret classification, the highest restricted category in the US system, lower levels being Secret and Confidential. It also appears that a DX (Direct Experimental) classification, related to priority over orders, materials and resources deemed an exceptional national urgency, was more effectively obtained for MX programmes.

Correctly, the DX rating should not apply to projects in this book, since it was not introduced before 8 September 1950 when it was part of the Defense Production Act begun in response to the start of the Korean War, essentially a partial mobilisation to an industry war-footing. It sought to prioritise controls over wage disputes and labour issues as well as securing access to rare materials, facilities and contractual arrangements for transport and other government facilities. In a rare application to a non-defence related activity, when it came along in the 1960s, NASA's Apollo Moon programme was granted a DX rating due to it being deemed an urgent national priority.

DX allocations are now made by the Defense Contract Management Agency (DCMA). The MX series was retained when the Materiel Division became the Air Materiel Command and proved to be a useful security classification with a fast-track to allocation. It spawned several subdivisions and frequently without any productive hardware or production programme. Over time there were attempts to retire it and AMC announced that it was to be abandoned, effective 1 July 1952, but in reality it lingered on for at least the next two years by which time it had reached MX-2276.

3
LIONS AND LAMBS

The end of the Second World War prompted dramatic changes in the way aircrew were recruited and trained. Air Training Command (ATC) went through dramatic reductions in personnel and facilities. On 29 November 1945 the Air Forces School was moved from Orlando, Texas, to Maxwell AFB, Alabama and 1 April 1946 it was renamed the Air University, also setting up the Air War College, the Air Command and Staff School and the Air Tactical School. But these were the headline items as the AAF shuffled around to find ways to maintain a proficient and well-trained Air Force.

The end of hostilities in Europe had immediately transferred priorities to preparation for the war against the Japanese mainland and all single-seater training took a back step as bomber crews got priority. It turned out that this was not necessary after the Japanese surrender on 15 August 1945 when Emperor Hirohito broadcast his acceptance of surrender terms, the first time the Japanese people had heard his voice, a fact which shocked many almost to disbelief that it was actually him.

In the rush to demobilise, the technical training establishments were shut down at such a rapid rate that it was difficult to keep pace with the closures, personnel frequently being asked to vacate a particular establishment without the senior officers knowing anything about such plans. The numbers speak for themselves. From 170 ATC bases at the end of 1944, just 140 remained by May 1945, reduced to 113 in September and a mere 34 by the end of the year. There then began one of the more bizarre episodes in the post-war history of the AAF.

By the end of 1945 the primary function of the ATC was to supervise the rapid separation of eligible personnel from the AAF and recruit Regular Army enlistees for operational duty in the post-war Air Force. In this way it was planned that the Air Force would be an entirely volunteer force and on 22 October it opened a Recruiting Section, preferably attracting experienced personnel with at least three years existing experience.

The figures too, speak for themselves. On 31 December 1943 the Air Training Command had 29,713 aircraft and 461,656 personnel of which 82,618 were civilians. At the end of 1944, the ATC boasted 21,052 training aircraft and 377,767 personnel including 100,841 civilians but by the end of 1945 it had only 6,169 aircraft and 136,134 personnel of whom 34,631 were civilians. By the end of 1946, it had 2,099 aircraft and 52,707 personnel of which 12,210 were civilians.

A companion *ab initio* trainer, the Boeing Model 75 Kaydet, or Stearman, trainer was a familiar sight at US air training fields and was adopted by many air forces, a not inconsiderable number remaining certificated for flight today. (Alan Wilson)

Wartime pilot training progressed to the North American BT-9, on which many post-war pilots had become familiar, its place in the peacetime Air Force taken by the AT-6. (NACA)

Successor to the BT-6, the AT-6 became the graduation trainer of choice for the new US Air Force. (USAAF)

Within a year of demobilisation and recruitment back in, a lot of skilled personnel were lost and techniques which had been developed at line-level on bases around the world were lost along with the experienced workforce. Moreover, an influx of new technologies during the last two years of the war, challenged recruits and young men – for exclusively men they were – without transition skills and basic engineering knowledge. In June 1946 pilot recruitment was set at 1,400 per year but that was impossible to achieve and it was lowered to 825 a few months later. By the end of the year only 325 pilots had passed through the system.

Across the AAF at large, the decision to achieve a post-war goal of 70 air groups proved unachievable in the parlous state of annual budgets for the Air Force and this was reduced to a planned 55 groups by 1 January 1948. This was achieved on paper but to fly the aircraft the ATC targeted an annual programme of 3,000 pilots. That challenge was brought to the attention of General Spaatz, the Air Force Chief of Staff, who insisted on the total being achieved. At group level, only by the most creative manipulation of the figures were the paper records available to future historians made to appear satisfied. A classic case of official records being a manipulated fudge, exposed through personal experiences and field records compared with official unit logs. By the end of 1947, ATC had 1,707 aircraft and 49,321 personnel, of which 8,677 were civilians.

The introduction of jet aircraft training began in 1946 but to ensure that there were adequate pilots for the new types, conversion courses were run only for commands already introducing these aircraft. Because the Air Force had not sought to develop two-seat jet fighters for training or conversion, the very different techniques in putting propeller-pilots in jet aircraft was dangerous and in early 1947 the 'captivair' device was introduced, an early form of simulator whereby aircraft were placed on poles to give pilots a realistic feel for the controls and operating procedures. This would be only a partial solution, veterans of the time informing this writer of its deficiencies. A more sustainable and valued asset was the two-seat T-33, introduced in 1948 as a stretched variant of the F-80 Shooting Star. It was with this that most fighter pilots would graduate from propeller-driven to jet-powered fighters and fighter-bombers.

A further casualty of cuts in resources saw a reduction in civilian personnel, most of whom were instructors and seasoned lecturers replaced by pilots who had only recently graduated themselves and had little or no practical experience. Moreover, very few were found to have any valuable teaching skills and lacked the incentive from a duty resented and bemoaned, all too frequently to sympathetic commanding officers supporting the view that the rightful place for a trained pilot was in the cockpit and not a classroom. The situation was made worse when a letter dated 17 September 1948 directed all commands to release many experienced personnel to support the Berlin Airlift. This brought a robust response asking the Pentagon which training bases they should close!

For much of 1948 there had been a productive awareness among the top brass that the entire Air Force would collapse unless something was done and a major reemployment programme for the civilian workforce began. By the end of the year the number of aircraft on hand had grown to 1,830 with 71,075 personnel of which 17,821 were civilian instructors and support personnel. It was not to last and for much of 1949 the Air Force, and especially the ATC, was in a period of heightened austerity. The Truman administration had decided that the Air Force could fulfil its mission with only 48 groups, down from the surge to 59 it had achieved the preceding year, and that a policy of expansion would be replaced by contraction.

The Department of Defense ordered major cuts in personnel and 25,000 civilian positions would be lost, 1,563 in Air Training Command alone. Flying hours were cut as were large numbers of reserve officers and rated personnel lowered to nonrated status with a consequent loss of pay. At the end of 1949 the official records attribute 2,132 aircraft and 70,752 personnel but only 12,710 civilians in that total, assimilation into other duties with the Air Force to show an actual loss of more than a quarter over the previous year.

The incoming Secretary of Defense Louis Johnson confirmed in office on 28 March 1949 was the chief executioner for the Truman White House and his advisers who were in open conflict with the Pentagon and the Air Force over ever-constrictive budget cuts and seemingly endless attempts to increase military unification and save tax dollars for a wave of other, domestic programmes. Johnson was forceful in 'demanding' that the Joint Chiefs of Staff at the Pentagon desist from public utterances questioning the logic of these cuts and force reductions. Only the previous year, the JCS Chief of Staff claimed that 'the Army of 1948 could not fight its way out of a paper bag'.

Coverage will be given in a separate series where the effect on naval aviation of the so-called 'Revolt of the Admirals' is considered, when Johnson mothballed most of the Navy's conventional fleet, scrapped other ships and, on 23 April

Over time, training aircraft would embrace the jet age, the Lockheed T-33 being an evolution from the two-seat F-80. (NMUSAF)

1949, cancelled the super-carrier USS *United States*. Suffice to say here that this greatly influenced the way the Air Force responded to the edict from the White House that all America needed for its defence would be a massive and unstoppable bomber force carrying atomic weapons to suppress and demoralise any attempt by aggressors to threaten the United States. That will be dealt with comprehensively in Volume 2 where the effect on procurement decisions pivoted on the B-36 contract.

While the ATC struggled to provide the pilots required by the civilian leadership, hotly contested by the uniformed services as implausible given the decreasing resources, there was a singularly progressive move on accepting women in the Air Force. On 12 June 1948, Congress had passed the Women's Armed Services Integration Act and in January 1950 the Officer Candidate School 49.V included the first WAF (Women's Air Force) into its course. But their numbers were limited to two percent of total military personnel and they were not to be assigned to combat duty. Not until 28 April 1993 were women in the USAF allowed to fly in combat.

A Volunteer Force

For most of the period covered by this volume, pilots were also inducted through the Aviation Cadet Training Program (AvCad), formed on 20 June 1941 when the US Army Air Forces (USAAF) succeeded the US Army Air Corps (USAAC). With it came the Aviation Cadet grade but this grew in May 1942 to also include trainee bombardiers and navigators with Moffett Field the first to set up a pre-flight training programme. Cadets received a basic monthly remuneration equivalent to $900/year. Average annual pay across the United States was $1,368 in 1940 rising to $1,885 two years later, equivalent in British money, using conversion values at the time, to £342 in 1940 and £471 in 1942. In the UK, the average annual wage at the time was about £250, or $1,000.

The cadets wore the same Army uniform but lacking the mohair cull of a full officer and the service cap had a blue hatband with the olive uniform, or brown with a khaki uniform. In almost all other respects the uniforms remained the same during a period of intense pressure on recruitment and training as the war expanded and the numbers of personnel grew almost exponentially. The training itself remained relatively unchanged from early 1942 and consisted of four stages, not counting the pre-flight stage originally set up at Moffett Field.

Recruits were subjected to a one-week classification stage where he would be assessed for training as a navigator, a bombardier or a pilot and then subjected to a tight physical examination with the sorry prospect of being sent to the regular Army if he failed. The pre-flight stage began with a six-week course to toughen up recruits and included athletics and military training, including tuition on procedures, processes and some familiarisation with the command structure. Then followed four weeks of academic study including general mechanics, the principles of flight and spot-courses on physics and mathematics with period tests for grading.

After passing those stages, cadets would be taught aeronautics and complex procedures calling for a lot of lateral thinking, including deflection shooting and working with three-dimensional situations, such as would be required for six-degrees of motion (up/down, left/right. back/forward) during aerial manoeuvres. After this the cadets were checked out on Link Trainers which simulated many aspects of real flying with an instructor for a one-hour session 'flying' an imaginary aircraft using basic controls duplicating those found in trainers. Created by Ed Link in 1929, the simulator had been used extensively by US pilot training programmes and those of many

Icons of Second World War fighter fame and relevant for building a tradition of Air Force service, Dominic Gentile (left) and Donald Blakeslee received the Distinguished Service Cross from General Dwight D Eisenhower on 11 April 1944. (USAAF)

Congresswoman Margaret Chase Smith was personally responsible for the Women's Armed Services Integration Act of 12 June 1948 which gave equal regular and reserve status for women in the military, doing much to enshrine in law the equality of opportunity afforded by the Constitution. (NARA)

other countries, becoming a familiar device for learning techniques and evaluating basic skills.

On completion of all these preliminary stages the cadets would be awarded cadet wings and sent to a primary pilot training course where a period of basic flying training would give them 60–65 hours experience in primary trainers, usually a Stearman or a Ryan type. These courses were run by the Civil Aeronautics Authority

War Training Service (CAA-WTS) operated by commercial organisations. From there, cadets would progress to a basic pilot training course where they would learn to fly over long distances, at night and in formation, flying on instruments or navigating by aerial procedures. They would add a further 70 flying hours in their logbooks on North American BT-9 or Vought BT-13 types.

Next up was the advanced pilot training course which would give cadets experience with either single-engine or multi-engine aircraft. Those assigned to single-engine aircraft would get checked out on the North American AT-6 advanced trainer while the rest would have a variety of different multi-engine aircraft on which to graduate and receive their pilot's wings. In both cases, pupils would log around 75–80 flying hours before going to transition pilot training where they would be assigned to fighters and fighter-bombers or bombers and transport types. In this phase they would receive two months training and type familiarisation before moving on to their assigned units.

There was a distinct hierarchy in that top graders would receive the rank of 2nd Lieutenants, graduates becoming flight officers but those who were unable to complete pilot training were sent off to navigator or bomb-aimer courses and if they failed there they would be sent to the flexible gunnery school. Cadet pilots who failed to pass basic or advanced training but were proficient on basic flying skills were assigned to reconnaissance, medevac or light transport units and known as liaison pilots, graded as flight officers.

The bombardier course lasted 18 weeks and required 425 hours of ground instruction followed by 120 flying hours completing proficiency tests from practice runs to live ordnance firing on bombing ranges. Graduates would receive their bombardier wings. Similarly, navigator and radio operator schools lasted 18 weeks with 500 hours of ground instruction preceding flying training and equipment familiarisation but the flexible gunnery school lasted six weeks and instructed personnel on how to operate gun turrets and flexible gun mounts. An interesting adjunct is that all aircrew had to do a course at gunnery school for use of that skill in emergencies.

A Leadership Quality

The establishment of an independent Air Force was central to defence thinking in the late 1940s and the academic training programmes set up in parallel to technical training sought to enhance the quality of leadership. That would be central to the expansion that was to follow the start of the Korean War in June 1950, when the policy of constraint and contraction was abandoned by necessity. The United States required a completely new level of airmanship but that also brought a need for a professional, career-based mentality and the possibility of promotion through merit. The challenges faced by aircrew in an age of great technical change were only one of the many new training needs but the crafting of a strong and effective leadership was critical to operational efficiency and to retaining personnel where civilian wages were outstripping service pay. So it was that a new culture was taught, one based on the need for a more sophisticated officer corps.

What the Air Force taught was that the ability to lead is not based on fear or the personal projection of position but rather on the degree to which those over whom the leadership has authority believes in the asserted mission of the group's purpose. So it is in politics as well as in the military; political leaders who cajole and 'instruct' the electorate are doomed to lose their trust and suffer at the ballot box; military leaders who exert authority through fear and punishment are doomed to get only lip-service from the rank and file, questioning every instruction as a grievance. Throughout political and military history, leaders achieve by projecting inspiration, asserting the value of the individual and the part he or she is called upon to play, or the level of their personal commitment.

These principles are taught to officer recruits in the Army, the Navy and the Air Force, instilling a sense of pride in projecting constrained management and authority while exuding confidence and a certainty of purpose. It is why the Air Force incorporated a strong history programme where leadership was taught by way of example from the lives of others, men such as Alexander the Great, Napoleon Bonaparte, Erwin Rommel, Dwight D Eisenhower and Winston Churchill, all of whom displayed an outstanding ability to attract loyalty to cause and perseverance in the face of adversity. And in more modern times, generals Pershing, Hoyt S Vandenberg and Carl Spaatz. Not for them the flaccid and patronising repetition of lies wrapped up as promises but a solid recognition of facts and realities which attract popular support through a sense of inclusivity within the 'bigger picture'.

The service of women in the AAF was acknowledged in 1945 but it would be three years before they achieved equality of status. In 1994 1st Lieutenant Jeannie M Flynn became the first female USAF fighter pilot, rising to command of the 4th FW at Seymour Johnson AFB, North Carolina. (NARA)

The Berlin Airlift of 1948–49 brought added roles to USAF fighter forces when Russian aircraft harried transport aircraft binging supplies of food and coal to the beleaguered city. (USAF)

So it was with leadership in the newly crafted United States Air Force as it leaned more strongly toward the precedent set by West Point and Annapolis. In the tradition of those establishments would emerge the Air Force Academy outside Colorado Springs, Colorado, but the foundation of that is found in the leaner days of the late 1940s when the mere survival of the Air Force as an independent arm of the military was questioned by some who had wanted to minimise its strength and to limit its capabilities, for the 'peace-dollar' they hoped to spend on other things.

A greater sense of identity was achieved through placing the value of the individual in the context of a tradition. The Air Force had that and sought to base training and the imperative of commitment as an inherent and implicit part of inducting recruits to its long history. The early American flyers went to war in 1917 with the purpose of joining an existing allied force deployed on the Western Front in a united effort against the German Army and its air service. That sense of identity which prevailed at the time grew during the interwar period and reached a peak in the Second World War.

Established on 12 March 1946, the Air University was set up to provide career-long education for Air Force personnel and evolved in the finest tradition of providing the uniformed serviceman with the highest level of academic learning at whatever level chosen. Located at Maxwell Field, renamed Maxwell Air Force Base with the formation of the USAF in September 1947, in 1949 it also became the home of archival records from the origin of military flying in the United States and became what is now the Air Force Historical Research Agency (AHRA). This emphasis on providing as comprehensive a record as possible of the history of the US Air Force has been connected with the keen desire to provide an alumni for serving members and for new inductees.

As the war ended with the surrender of Japan, General Arnold asked Edward Peck Curtis, an ace of the First World War and a senior officer during the Second World War, to form an organisation

Legacy long-range fighter of the Second World War, the Lockheed P-38 Lightning served in every theatre of the Second World War and would serve with the Air Force until 1949, although 1,887 had been cancelled when peace came. (USAF)

to knit together past and present members of the Air Force and its precursors in what was quickly formed as the US Air Force Association (AFA). It came into being on 4 February 1946 not only as a veteran's organisation but as an advocacy for air power and for standards to ensure the best possible provision for the airman's lot. It quickly faced opposition as a politically-orientated body which the Navy in particular saw as a lobbying group for higher Air Force budgets and seeking priority over its own requirements. In several respects it was – and proudly so by the AFA's mission statement! But the real mission of the organisation ran deeper still.

The twin-boom arrangement of the P-38 had an impact on other aircraft designs, tests providing partial solutions to the problem of compressibility close to the transonic and notably the wing which was the basis for that employed on the Lockheed Constellation. (USAF)

The projection of the fighter pilot as the epitome of defence ran counter to the national defence policy of deterrence through the use of massed bomber formations but in the public mind the 'leatherneck' heroes of recent warfare and fighting in the 'wild blue yonder' were the front-line of national protection. The AFA recognised this and courted Hollywood moguls for films embodying the daredevil antics of imaginary fighter pilots. It acted as intermediary connecting directors and movie producers with the Air Force leadership, receiving permission for access to bases and Air Force facilities. Thus did the organisation play no small part in shaping the way the Air Force in general was seen by the American public who, through those channels, received as distorted a view of the fighter pilot as they did of the Old West depicted on television screens across the nation.

To accompany the image of daring duellists in cloud-studded skies, in 1947 Robert MacArthur Crawford penned lyrics to a tune put together in 1939 and which was first called the 'Army Air Corps' but which became 'Army Air Forces' in 1941 and finally the 'US Air Force' in 1947, a song more popularly known as the 'Wild Blue Yonder' from the first line of the lyric. It has become immortalised in this world and on another, being the instrumental tune switched on when astronauts Scott and Irwin lit up their Lunar Module Ascent Stage on 2 August 1972 to leave the lunar surface and begin their journey home.

1st Lieutenant H A Blood inspects the ammunition belts and feed trays on the P-38, a configuration which unsurprisingly became the template for nose armament on the P-80 Shooting Star, another way in which this one aircraft became a transition exemplar for the new jet fighters coming into service in the immediate post-war years. (USAF)

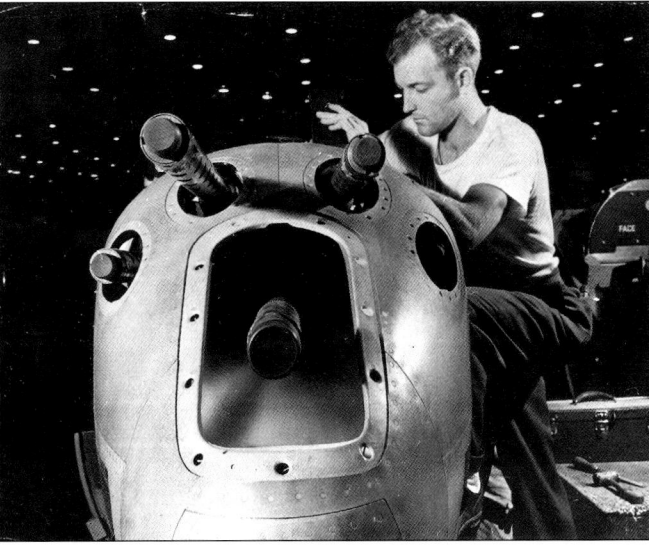

Aircraft armament would evolve only slowly in the US Air Force and in future engagements would be considered inadequate during air-to-air-combat when Soviet aircraft had more effective firepower. (NARA)

4
FIGHTERS FOR THE FORCE

At the end of 1945, the Army Air Forces had 16,799 fighters on hand at home and abroad, the vast majority being the propeller-driven types which would gradually transition to jet fighters throughout this period up to 1949. Development of jet aircraft had been underway since 1942 and before the end of the war industry had already produced several experimental types (see Appendix). What follows are the new aircraft which would achieve operational status before the end of 1949, or types which were key contributors to US air power in this period. Presented in chronological order of first flight and according to their service designations they include 'P' numbers which were incidental to the mainstream development of fighters and others which may be found in the Appendix.

The transition from piston-engine to jet engine was rapid and caused major new technologies to suddenly emerge to meet the requirements. Examination of the figures requires care since what were labelled 'aircraft engines' were also made available for use in tanks and some other armoured fighting vehicles. So the company production returns are no guide and have proven to be misleading in several documents and books recording the quantities used in the aviation industry.

Of those in that latter category, US manufacturers delivered 815,238 engines between the beginning of 1940 and the end of 1946 but in the last three years of that period a total 369,186 were delivered of which 2,259, 0.6 percent were jet engines. However, the total number of aero-engines produced in 1946 was only 2,624 of which 929 were jet engines, 35.4 percent. In 1949 authorisation was granted to the Air Force for procurement of 2,324 airframes of which 1,457 (62.7 percent) were for fighter types, all of which were powered by jet engines.

By the end of 1949, on a paper inventory the Air Force had 17,686 aircraft, down from 20,572 at the end of March that year, of which 3,862 were fighters. Of those, 1,967 were piston-types, about half the inventory being powered by jet engines of which the majority were F-80s. Moderating conclusions drawn by these figures, it should be noted that Air Force records show a total active inventory of 12,319 aircraft in June 1949, including 8,716 with the full-time Air Force, 949 with reserve units and 2,654 with the Air National Guard (ANG). Of the total 3,862 fighters on paper, 1,973 were inactive due to a variety of reasons most notable of which were repairs, modifications, aircraft on maintenance or in reserved, non-flyable condition pending work.

This was the first year in which line allocations were separated into functional categories and unit inventories do not always match the service inventory. By the time reported totals worked their way up to Air Force HQ the totals had changed again down at field level. The figures quoted here may vary from other published sources but are drawn from returns by individual units and therefore present a snapshot across the Air Force and not at a level claimed at HQ in official histories. The difference between numerical force-levels and the actual combat-ready inventories always reflects a delay caused by the speed with which the bureaucracies respond and that can be several weeks. The unit levels reflect actual versus theoretical capabilities and readiness levels.

Another measure of effective operational capability is the age of the force and at the end of 1949 fewer than half the inventory

An official poster of the US Army Air Forces during the Second World War extolls the capabilities of the P-38 Lightning, precursor to a succession of recruitment aids when, toward the late 1940s the need for an expanded Air Force became apparent, if not immediately affordable. (USAAF)

were less than 54 months old, all of which were jets. There was also a significant drawdown in airfields, a total of 207 still active in 1949 with a further 152 overseas, of which only 96 were active. The reduction in overseas bases was indicative of the prevailing foreign policy of the United States during the Truman administration and in the period before the Korean War began in June 1950.

Many deactivated bases outside the United States remained derelict due to the cost of returning unused facilities to agricultural land. This was particularly the case in Britain, where the parlous state of the national economy prevented expenditure and manpower on work necessary to remove vast expanses of concrete and numerous unwanted buildings. Much of this backlog never was addressed and many places today, both in Britain and abroad, retain the ground infrastructure built during the Second World War, sometimes repurposed by the landowners.

Another element of the changing requirements was the need for scientific research and development at a fundamental level to support

Air Force operations and ensure maximum use of new technology, particularly as it related to jet engines and fighter aircraft. The first specified category for a Research and Development Command was established in 1949, the first time the Air Force had its own budget line-item for this work. Funding for such programmes increased from $145 million in 1948 to $225 million the following year and $233 million in 1950. Much of this went to industry, with the major airframe, engine and equipment suppliers being contracted for specific research and development projects.

Requirements

The United States Army Air Forces and the US Navy faced major decisions regarding the future of air policy, planning, requirements and specifications. Jet engines were clearly the way of the future for all combat aircraft and early imperfections, poor reliability and low performance were recognised as teething troubles which would be weaned out as experience in design and operation increased. But there were certain imperatives to guide air policy, not least those gleaned from combat operations since America entered the war in December 1941.

As the Second World War moved toward victory against Nazi Germany and Imperial Japan, in early 1945 the AAF considered post-war requirements for a peacetime air force and focused on three priorities: a long-range escort fighter for bombers; the development of jet aircraft to fill a wide range of roles; and an all-weather capability for air defence and ground attack. This latter requirement had gained traction during the disastrous early phase of the Battle of the Bulge in December 1944 when German troops retook previously secured ground in the Ardennes in the absence of Allied air cover due to extensive fog, mist and snow.

From existing and more general experience operating aircraft in hostile climates, problems defending far-northern locations were made difficult when poor weather and freezing conditions kept conventional aircraft grounded. Defence of northernmost areas such as Alaska prompted the AAF's Requirements Division to issue a request on 23 March 1945 for an all-weather fighter-bomber specifically designed to guard the northern borders under such conditions. Initially, it required a piston-engine type to replace the P-61 Black Widow but that December it changed the requirement to a jet-powered aircraft.

That requirement was defined through a specification issued by the Air Technical Service Command (ATSC) during July and August 1945 when general characteristics were evaluated. Raising concerns at specific conclusions about particular requirements, in September the Assistant Chief of the Air Staff set up a review to establish operational needs. Various senior AAF commanders testified regarding their individual perceptions on requirements, as well as consultation with Army commanders in charge of ground operations with experience in operating with air support. After those conversations, it concluded that the requirements should be as forward-looking as practical and that the same high standards for wartime characteristics should be retained.

It also advised that the type of weapons selected should focus on futuristic systems, rejecting the .50-in (1.27cm) machine gun for possibilities raised with weapons of higher calibre and with a capability for air-to-air rockets and missiles. This requirement was implemented after the specifications for the P-80 Shooting Star, the P-84 Thunderjet and the F-86 Sabre had been written and readers will note from the following entries for fighter types that weapons of this calibre were carried by all three types. But the Air Staff wanted a more futuristic conceptual approach rather than retaining the weapons and armament of the then existing conflict. The requirements established three fighter types for post-war development, including a penetration fighter, an interceptor fighter and an all-weather fighter, with the latter considered a priority.

The penetration fighter was to have two gas turbine engines, each with a thrust of 3,000lb (13.34kN) set in an airframe of minimum size and weight and located close together to avoid undue asymmetry of control in the event of one shutting down. The aircraft would be required to conduct steep dives and be fitted with dive brakes, with armament being six .50-in machine guns, four .60-in calibre guns or four 20mm cannon. This requirement was to underpin the design of the XF-88 and the XF-90 (see Appendix).

The interceptor requirement departed from convention by stipulating rocket motors as the sole means of propulsion and deferred specific performance to industry proposals. The concept was greatly influenced by German research projects as they became known immediately after the war in Europe, which had stimulated much of the rethink since March 1945. Weapons were to be four .50-in calibre machine guns.

The all-weather fighter would be a larger aircraft than required for the preceding two categories, if only because of the need for a powerful radar in the nose, a second crewmember as radar/weapons operator and fuel sufficient for a relatively long range in addition to armament for combat. Power would be provided by two gas turbine engines mounted in the fuselage, although propellers were considered a possible option with some favouring the use of turboprop engines for low-altitude work. Weapons were to be six .60-in calibre machine guns or six 20mm cannon. The aircraft requirement issued on 23 March 1945 would result in the F-89 Scorpion and in the F-94 Starfire.

These characteristics were circulated to existing airframe companies on 6 August 1945, with responses from 13 manufacturers. The only big player absent was Boeing, its design teams fully active with a range of new bomber proposals and development work on existing types such as the B-50. Criteria for assessing bids would

By 1949 the Western Allies and NATO in particular faced down the challenge posed by a belligerent Soviet Union, with challenges from the air focusing on cross-Arctic routes which bombers would traverse in both directions linking respective continents. (Author's collection)

rate the company's financial status and its corporate management structure, physical capacity to carry out the work and the technical resilience of its proposal.

There was an inclination to go with major manufacturers with a proven record while newcomers would be chosen only if their design had clearly superior qualities. The AAF wanted to retain long-standing manufacturers with large networks of ancillary supply chains ensuring a comprehensive labour market and smooth production lines. There was considerable emphasis on awarding contracts to balance the different financial and work backlogs between contenders so that those with lean order-books could be prioritised. Redefined, the military characteristics of the three categories were reissued on 23 November 1945.

The following entries describe fighter aircraft with first flights by 31 December 1949, coverage depending on the influence of respective types prior to this date and likely to be continued in subsequent volumes covering later periods. It also covers fighter types of different categories which flew before the end of the Second World War but were also of significance in the period 1945–1949.

Bell P-59 Airacomet; First flight: 2 October 1942
The latter stages of the Second World War saw several projects testing the capabilities of the new jet engine and high-speed flight for escort and interception roles. To help prepare for that future the Bell P-59 Airacomet was the company's first jet fighter, which made its first hop on 1 October 1942 with a formal first flight the following day. It was powered by two General Electric J31 engines, a domestic US build of the Power Jets W.1 provided by the British through a deal negotiated by General Arnold.

This was the first US jet combat aircraft, primarily developed as a research project with combat capability very firmly in second place. Nevertheless, the programme would help Bell obtain a subsequent contract for a transonic research aircraft, the X-1. Bell had developed a respectable reputation for innovative designs and was considered a safe candidate to begin development of a jet prototype.

In July 1941 the AAF had issued an Advanced Development Objectives (ADO) list of technology programmes it considered priority for early exploitation among which was the turbojet engine

A single 37mm cannon and three 0.50-in machine guns armed the largely unsuccessful attempt to make the P-59 America's first operational jet fighter, which it never became. Note the large chin inlets blended into the fuselage sides and underwing positions in this view of a P-59B. (USAF)

being actively developed in Italy, Germany and Britain. The first jet aircraft, the German Heinkel He 178 had flown for the first time on 27 August 1939 followed by the British Gloster E.28/39 on 15 May 1941 and the German Me 262 with a jet engine on 18 July 1942.

In a meeting held at Wright Field on 4 September 1941 the General Electric Corporation had been asked to build the W.1 under licence. The next day Bell, with its facility in close proximity to General Electric (GE), received a request to build a suitable aircraft via a contract for three aircraft (42-108784, 42-108785 and 42-108786), signed on 9 January 1942. The entire programme was Top Secret and the cover designation XP-59A was applied, inferring that it was a development of the XP-59, a pusher-fighter which had been cancelled on 1 December 1941.

The rapid rise of GE as the prime jet engine builder of this period came upon the company by way of Stanford Moss, an expert in turbo-supercharger design, and a skilled technologist, Dale Streid who had at first been highly sceptical of jet turbine engines

The first jet fighter built by Bell Aircraft, the P-59 Airacomet borrowed design and production practices honed by the company on other aircraft projects including the P-39 Airacobra to make its first flight 11 months after America entered the Second World War. The aircraft shown here is the YP-59A. (USAF)

until he was given access to Whittle's work. Whittle had presented a paper titled 'Airplane Propulsion by Means of a Jet reaction and Gas Turbine Power Plant' and that inspired Streid who teamed with Moss on some theoretical concepts.

Due to concerns about security as the AAF pitched in to development of jet aircraft, very little information about the Whittle engine or the GE derivative was passed along to Bell so engineers designed a conservative aircraft adopting a cantilever, laminar-flow wing for optimum efficiency and a retractable tricycle undercarriage. It featured a high-set, horizontal tailplane well clear of the jet efflux from the two engines which were carried in nacelles blended to the underside wing roots. The prototypes had GE I-A engines each delivering a thrust of 1,400lb (5.12kN). Pleased with the result, in March 1942 the AAF ordered 13 pre-production YP-59As with the more powerful I-16/J31 turbojets with a thrust of 1,650lb (6.04kN).

The first XP-59A was followed into the air by the second aircraft on 15 February 1943 and the third about five weeks later. Although an experimental concept demonstrator, the XP-59A was overweight from engines which turned out to be heavier than expected, underpowered and relatively unstable in flight. The AAF had wanted it to serve as precursor to a fully-fledged combat aircraft and had fitted armament in the nose but with the disappointing performance that was not possible. Moreover, the engines were unreliable and frequently shed turbine blades with predictable results.

The first YP-59A became airborne in August 1943 and showed virtually no improvement and the third (42-22611) was sent to England for analysis at the Royal Aircraft Establishment (RAE) in exchange for the first production Gloster Meteor F.1 (EE210). Tested at Farnborough, the YP-59A failed to impress and demonstrated that at this stage the Americans were some way behind the British, both in design and in the technology of jet-powered aircraft. Evaluated against the Gloster E.28/39, the Meteor and the de Havilland Vampire, the RAE found serious flaws but some, such as a long take-off run and low acceleration were shared with most jets of the period. The US Navy got the eighth and ninth production aircraft (42-108778 and 42-108779) but found it totally unsuited to potential carrier operations. The AAF had ordered 50 production aircraft just before the first flight of the XP-59A but with no potential for operational service as a fighter, all but 30 were cancelled.

In subsequent flight trials against the P-47D and the P-38J, the XP-59As performed badly and they were suitable only as experimental research aircraft but that judgement opened the door to the Lockheed P-80, designed from the outset as a combat aircraft. Bell's work had provided the baseline from which engine and airframe designs could evolve into first-generation fighters. The performance of the British experimental aircraft and the known performance of the German jets gave urgency to the need for a suitable contender to engage with the enemy on at least equal terms.

A cutaway I-16/J31 turbojet engine of the type developed from the Whittle engine which powered the P-59 when it entered a brief period of service with the first activated jet fighter squadron, the 412th. Note the censor has blanked out the serial number. (USAF)

Only 66 aircraft of this type were built, of which 20 were the P-59A and 30 were the P-59B. The Airacomet served with the 412th FG for familiarisation and test purposes. The definitive P-59B had a more powerful J31-GE-5 centrifugal turbojet engine delivering a thrust of 2,000lb (8.9kN) supporting a top speed of 413mph (664km/hr) and a maximum range of 375 miles (604km).

The 412th had been formed at Muroc Army Air Field, California, on 29 November 1943, located six miles (9.6km) from the Rogers Dry Lake bed. On 11 March 1944 Airacomet testing began with the 445th FS after which the group relocated to Palmdale Army Air Field, California, where the 29th FS and 31st FS joined it. The original plan had been to carry out tests with the jet as part of IV Fighter Command. The 412th has its place in history as the first US jet fighter squadron activated and trials with the P-59A were conducted in close connection with Bell and its engineers and technicians. It would shortly be joined by Lockheed personnel bringing in the XP-80 Shooting Star.

A P-59B (44-22650), of the variant introduced in 1947 as the first US combat type to have a built-in ejection seat. This particular aircraft was delivered prior to the bulk contract cancellation at the end of the war and spent some time with the NACA before being delivered to the National Museum of the US Air Force. (NMUSAF)

Table 1: Bell P-59 Airacomet Specifications

	XP-59	XP-59A	YP-59A	P-59A
Span	40ft/12.19m	45.5ft/13.87m	49ft/14.94m	45.5ft/13.87m
Length	37.25ft/11.35m	38.16ft/11.63m	38.16ft/11.63m	38.83ft/11.84m
Height	12ft/3.66m	12.3ft/3.76m	12ft/3.66m	12ft/3.66m
Empty weight	7,960lb/3,611kg	7,320lb/3,320kg	7,626lb/3,459kg	7,950lb/3,606kg
Gross weight	10,463lb/4,746kg	n/a	10,532lb/4,777kg	10,822lb/4,909kg
Max speed	450mph/724kph	404mph/650kph	409mph/658kph	413mph/665kph
Ceiling	38,000ft/11,582m	n/a	43,200ft/13,167m	46,200ft/14,082m
Range	850mls/1,358km	n/a	640mls/1,030km	375mls/604km

Lockheed P/F-80 Shooting Star; First flight: 8 January 1944

Since 1939 when it began supplying the British, the Lockheed Aircraft Corporation had produced 19,273 aircraft for the war effort, seeing its payroll increase from 332 people in 1934 to 7,900 in 1939 and a peak of 90,853 in 1943, before falling to 17,156 by the end of 1946. In all, it produced 9,924 P-38 Lightning fighters, further orders being cancelled on VJ Day. With a significant future ahead as a major supplier of fighter aircraft for the Air Force, it had an appropriately auspicious start. As with all manufacturers, after the war Lockheed had to lay off a large number of its workforce but the company had the P-80 on the production line as the AAF's first credible jet fighter.

A Lockheed P-80B (44-85004) displaying the smoothly blended fuselage and low wing setting with integral intakes at the root for a single J33 turbojet engine. (USAF)

Lockheed had a habit of looking more to the future than the present and benefitted from the persistent interest in the potential from jet engines by Hall Hibberd, chief of the engineering design department, and Clarence 'Kelly' Johnson. These two had worked on the concept since 1939 and had Nathan Price outline a suitable design for a jet aircraft. Given the company number L-1000, the engine failed to deliver and the aircraft, the Model L-133 was unable to get funding from the AAF, who had a distinctly conservative approach regarding new and untried concepts. Circulated to Wright Field on 24 February 1942, the Lockheed L-111/L-133 attracted little interest.

By early 1943 General Arnold was receiving uncomfortable news, for while the Republic P-47 was entering service, facing the *Luftwaffe*'s Focke-Wulf Fw 190 and the new variants of the Messerschmitt Bf 109, the jet-powered Me 262 and imminent trials with the rocket-powered Me 163 were progressing fast. Moreover, on 5 March 1943 the British had flown their first jet fighter, the Gloster Meteor, and were nearing flight trials with the de Havilland Vampire, which would occur on 20 September.

Against this backdrop, and with the anticipation of significantly more intense air combat and bombing operations over occupied Europe in the coming months, pressure applied by General Arnold supported this new generation of aircraft. The YP-59A pre-production Airacomet was coming up for its own flight trials but the pace of development with the British and German projects shook off apathy. The reluctance of the AAF to get involved in advanced concepts evaporated in the face of new threats from an enemy already spending vast sums of money on advanced research and development projects, much of which was known to the Allies.

As a result, the story of America's first truly successful jet combat aircraft began on 17 May 1943 when Brigadier General Franklin O Carroll, then the chief of the Army Air Forces Engineering Division, convened a team and gathered recommendations from discussions held several weeks earlier. Those had taken place between Lockheed engineers and managers and the Air Technical Service Command. Lockheed had been asked to submit a proposal for a fighter which would maximise the potential of the de Havilland Halford H.1B turbojet engine. Quickly afterwards, Lockheed started the L-140 programme and on 17 June 1943 the AAF approved it, following the decision to proceed with its development as the XP-80.

Speed was of the essence, both to show the company was ahead of the competition and to fill requirements for an early demonstration. Some cooperation had been evident when in late 1942 the Air Technical Service Command had passed to Lockheed the drawings of the Bell XP-59B and followed that the following March with the drawings of the H.1B turbojet engine along with specifications and the materials inventory. The AAF awarded the XP-80 contract on 17 June and that was approved exactly seven days later for what was also designated MX-409. Suggested first by Lockheed as a deadline to deliver, the AAF concurred that the company had 180 days from the date of the contract to design and build the first prototype. It would be ready seven days short of that.

Johnson formed a small team assisted by William P Ralston and Don Palmer operating a six-day per week work schedule from a small building close to the wind tunnel at Plant B-1. People were brought in as required and at peak the group had 23 engineers and 105 assembly technicians on hand. Secrecy was of the essence, as it was for the entire jet engine development programme across all manufacturers and government facilities. Even the NACA was kept

A flight line of P-80A Shooting Star fighters, the nearest aircraft (44-85142) being converted into a photo-reconnaissance type. (USAF)

By this date the mock-up had been inspected when a 12-man team from the AAF, a representative from the Navy and two RAF officers from the British Air Commission spent three days, 20–22 July, visiting Lockheed's Burbank facility. From this flowed acceptance with only minor changes and the XP-80 was given its serial number, 44-83020. Delays to the engine prompted consideration of an alternative, the less powerful General Electric I-16 rather than the H-1B which under licence would receive the US designation Allis Chalmers J36.

At the time, Lockheed opposed the idea of the I-16 and in September it proposed the L-141 version of the XP-80 design which would be powered by the more powerful General Electric I-40 engine, eventually built by Allis Chalmers and GE as the J33. This concept was accepted by the AAF as the XP-80A and a contract placed on 16 February 1944, indicative of how the definitive fighter concept was wrapped around available engines. Gas turbine engines were the pacing item and the driving technology for the jet combat aircraft which would emerge from the existing propulsion systems, the key to which was the availability of the British engines.

at arm's length as the Air Force wanted industry to build the jet and not just assemble a group of research scientists. The AAF had always been suspicious that, if left in charge of a military development project, the NACA would always bend it into a research programme, jeopardising its operational function as a combat aircraft.

At Lockheed, this team began what would later be known as the Skunk Works and provide a progressively more advanced series of projects for the Air Force through to the present. But in 1943 the company was in the midst of a massive ramp-up in existing production quotas and gearing hard for a significant increase in the war effort. Lockheed President Robert Gross and Hall Hibberd delegated control of the jet programme to Johnson, even then considered one of the bright stars in the company design office. He began by compiling a countdown diary showing days remaining to the required completion date!

Johnson's approach was to achieve efficiency through simplicity and the team opted for a low aspect ratio, laminar-flow wing in a clean configuration overall. The engine was located in the centre fuselage section with wing root intakes situated forward and in the lower fuselage. On 10 July, the team received its first Whittle engine, flown in by Air Transport Command, although this was only a mock-up preceding a complete working engine. That was delayed due to test problems in Britain but it finally arrived on 2 November 1943, a non-flyable 'installation' engine.

The intensity of the work schedule and size of the load carried by this small team had its effect on the health of the engineers and technicians, an unusually high number of days being lost due to illness recorded on the daily logs and particularly in Johnson's meticulous diary. The pressure on the company was high, with the P-51 Mustang and the added seclusion of this Top Secret group raising levels of workload and very long days. Just one more tranche of pressure placed on Johnson as he managed an increasingly demanding set of schedules and supply management.

A line-up of P-80As of the 1st FG as the Shooting Star played a seminal role in bringing the jet age to the US Air Force, a type well suited to this initial phase of jet fighter roles but which would quickly be eclipsed by more capable successors. (USAF)

On 17 November a test was conducted on the 2,460lb (10.9kN) thrust H.1B engine during which the two air ducts collapsed at an engine speed of 800rpm, sucking debris into the impellers and causing damage. A second engine arrived on 28 December and was ground tested with redesigned ducts. The prototype had six .50-in machine guns with 200 rounds per gun and two wing and one fuselage tanks, all self-sealing, with an unpressurised cockpit and a sliding bubble canopy. By now the aircraft had been nicknamed *Lulu Belle* and was declared ready for its first flight. That took place on 8 January 1944 with Milo Burcham at the controls, take-off occurring at 9:10am. It lasted only six minutes due to a failure of the landing gear retract switch and Burcham was quickly back in the air for 20 minutes giving an impressive display of the aircraft's speed and agility, buzzing the Muroc control tower and demonstrating a roll rate of 360 degrees/second.

The accessible armament troughs for the P-80 with the cover doors open showing the feed trays and ammunition belts for the six 0.50-calibre machine guns. (USAF)

Over the next few flights several problems were noted, appreciably the poor stall and spin characteristics and several adjustable issues with fuel management and some control forces. But the engine itself was the main problem, although that would eventually be solved by better understanding of operating procedures although the aircraft itself had grown in size and capability. Nevertheless, XP-80 demonstrated a top speed of 502mph (808km/hr) at an altitude of 20,480ft (6,240m). Early trials were undertaken by Lockheed test pilots but five weeks after the first flight the Air Force began to increasingly take charge of the tests, Captain W A Lien piloting the XP-80 on 12 February, its sixth trial flight.

An improved variant

Development of the aircraft began with the contract for two XP-80As (44-83021 and 44-83022) ordered in early 1944. Larger and powered by a 4,000lb (17.79kN) thrust General Electric I-40 (J33-GE) engine further aft, overall length was increased from 32.9ft (10m) to 34.5ft (10.5m) with a wingspan increased from 37ft (11.2m) to 39ft (11.8m). The wing area was reduced slightly due to a modest reduction in the chord. With maximum weight increased from 8,916lb (4,044kg) to 13,780lb (6,250kg), modifications were made to the landing gear. Equipped with six .50-in machine guns, the nose contained 250 rounds per gun and fuel capacity was increased from 285USgal to 485USgal. The second XP-80A carried a 165USgal drop tank underneath each wing tip, which would become standard on production aircraft.

Work on the first of two XP-80As began on 2 January 1944 (prior to the contract award) as the L-141 project and on 21 January at a meeting chaired by Johnson it was decided to separate the development of the XP-80A and the 23 YP-80 pre-production aircraft along with a static test article to a different division of Lockheed. Ralston was to move the programme out from the Skunk Works as it began to slip into the assembly phase. Three days later, Johnson's log identified 24 January as a full-scale start on the L-141/XP-80A. The first I-40 engine arrived on 27 April, the two XP-80As being the first American aircraft to have US-built engines. Painted light grey, it was named *Gray Ghost*. It departed Burbank for Muroc and the NACA test facility at 3:20am, 4 June 1944. Filmed by AAF cameramen, this was the first time the P-80 programme had been exposed to public view, and then only through newsreels.

Piloted by Tony Le Vier, XP-80A 83021 made its first flight on 10 June 1944 and in subsequent tests the type was found to have a 'buzz' during high-speed runs which tunnel tests and NACA investigation discovered could be due to the compressibility wall around Mach 0.8. It was solved by tightening the tension of the control cables. But the engine was still not perfected and the fuel supply system was inadequate, consumption was totally unacceptable and the revs had to be kept lower than rated to keep it running. Worst of all, there was a five-hour limit on running the turbine. Tests also revealed the need for a boundary-layer bleed for the air intakes but the taller vertical tail maintained directional stability. Technicians liked the detachable aft fuselage section which allowed much better access to the engine and tailpipe.

On 20 March 1945 the engine on the first XP-80A disintegrated and the aircraft broke up. LeVier escaped with only back injuries incurred when he took to his parachute. The fault was eventually discovered after the turbine wheel that had fractured was eventually found by a farmer a year later about six miles (9.6km) from where the incident had occurred. The wheel was found to contain a concentration of metallurgical impurities from a single ingot. The second aircraft was modified and a second seat installed in the tight enclosure so that an engineer could conduct inflight tests with the J34 engine, which was also destined for the XF-90. That necessitated a spine across the top of the fuselage to carry the fuel lines for an afterburner, which was not fitted to this aircraft.

Completed in July 1944, the second XP-80A (44-83022) was delivered to Muroc by truck, left unpainted so that its pure performance could be compared with *Gray Ghost*. Nicknamed *Silver Ghost*, Tony LeVier took it up for the first time on 1 August 1944 and with space for an engineer it was dedicated to engine tests with a view to getting the issues sorted out for the production aircraft. To do that a large number of instruments were attached for measuring thrust, intake pressures, exhaust temperatures and fuel consumption levels at specific revs. In addition, the dorsal fin accommodated additional instrumentation.

On 10 March 1944 the AAF had ordered 13 YP-80A pre-production aircraft (44-83023 to 44-83035) powered by the I-40 turbojet engine which carried the service designation J33-GE-9, or the GE-11 according to specification. They were essentially the same as the XP-80As. The first YP-80A took to the skies on 13 September for a start to the manufacturer's trials, 44-83023 going to the NACA's Moffett Field facility six days later for a series of tests where, specially instrumented, it would be put through a rigorous evaluation. Focused mainly on high-speed diving trials, those tests continued up to 27 January 1947. However, keen to get the P-80, now named Shooting Star by Robert Gross and Hall Hibberd, into operational evaluation as soon as possible, the AAF laid plans to send some of these pre-production types over to the UK and Europe.

It was always going to be a taxing aircraft to fly, pilots learning the vicissitudes of first-generation jets the hard and brutal way. But the challenges facing Lockheed and the AAF were painfully self-evident during its first years of service and flight evaluations. A series of catastrophic accidents began with the crash of the third YP-80A on 20 October 1944 when the engine flamed out after the turbopump failed, killing the Lockheed test pilot Milo Burcham. The cause was identified, a corrective procedure implemented and, with the war raging to a new intensity following the breakout in France after the D-Day landings, four aircraft were sent to get a feel for jet combat.

The fourth and fifth YP-80As were sent to RAF Burtonwood, England in December 1944 but the first crashed on 28 January 1945 during its second flight, killing Major Frederick Borsodi. The second aircraft was delivered to Rolls-Royce where it received an RB.41 engine, the prototype of the Nene. That was heavily damaged and written off following a crash-landing after an engine failure at Syerston on 14 November 1945. The wreckage was delivered to Burtonwood. The sixth and seventh aircraft (44-83028 and -82029) were sent to Italy where they were to be evaluated under combat conditions, as much for the benefit of the ground crews and handling personnel as the pilots.

They arrived in late December 1944, survived the experience and were returned to the United States to be flown by personnel from Wright Field, ending up with the 1st FG before that unit was disbanded on 16 October 1945, one eventually being modified into a target drone. The second aircraft had the same history but was lost in a crash at Brandenburg, Kentucky, on 2 August 1945 killing the pilot. The 10th YP-80A (44-83032) had a varied career with several units within the 412th FG but it too had already crashed, at the same airfield on 9 July 1945 due to engine failure. The last YP-80A was also destroyed in a crash.

In all, five of the 13 YP-80As had been lost to engine failures, a product of the nascent jet industry and not the inherent design of the aircraft. The crash ratio was not very different to other first-generation jet aircraft, where a similar experience revealed a lot of learning still to be acquired in the development, installation and operation of gas turbine engines in combat aircraft. The performance of the aircraft itself was encouraging and production orders had been issued on 4 April 1944 for two batches of 500 aircraft, with a further order for an additional 2,500 aircraft awarded in April 1945. These were designated P-80A-LO, adopting the 'F' prefix when that change was introduced in June 1948. With the surrender of Japan, the first order for 1,000 aircraft was cut back to 917, which would be designated P-80A and P-80B.

Seeking to obtain a photographic reconnaissance version, on 23 September 1944 the AAF ordered that the second of this batch (44-83024) was to be adapted for such purpose and redesignated XF-14, the 'F' reflecting the PR designation of the time. Modifications included the removal of the nose guns, replaced with a set of cameras and a window built in to the underside of the fuselage forward of the landing leg. It was destroyed on 6 December 1944 during a night flight when it collided with a B-25 Mitchell (44-29120) near Muroc AB. Added to the other YP-80As lost, that brought to six the total crashes.

The first 345 P-80A aircraft were powered by either the 3,850lb (17.12kN) J33-GE-11 engine or the J33-A-9 built by the Allison Division of General Motors. The next 218 aircraft received the 4,000lb (17.79kN) thrust J33-A-17 which featured a boundary-layer control splitter plate in the air intake and this more powerful engine was retrofitted into the earlier production models when they became available. On 19 January 1945 North American had been granted a production order for 1,000 P-80As which would have been designated P-80N but this was a component of the order for 2,500 cancelled after VJ Day.

Intensely proud of its capabilities and ever keen to project performance through speed, range and the fighting capabilities of its aircraft, the AAF was ruffled by the world speed record achieved by an RAF Gloster Meteor F.4 (EE454 *Britannia*) piloted by Wing Commander H J Wilson on 11 November 1945 at a speed of 606.38mph (975.66km/hr). The Lockheed Skunk Works was approached with a request to determine whether a P-80A could be modified to get the record back. Johnson quickly assured the AAF that in his estimation a speed of 615mph (989.5km/hr) could be achieved and with very little modification. For a predicted speed of 635mph (1,021.7km/hr) it would require flush air intakes, squared wing tips, water-alcohol injection for the engine and a sharper wing leading-edge. Arnold agreed to fund both modified and unmodified options.

A P-80 (44-85064) of the 1st FG posed for a view with the aft fuselage separated from the forward section and the J33 turbojet engine suspended by an extraction hoist. The ability to remove the engine through a split-fuselage separation line would be adopted by other aircraft of the period. (USAF)

The Need for Speed

Under the eagle-eyed scrutiny of monitors from the *Fédération Aéronautique Internationale* (FAI), the AAF conducted several runs with a P-80A specifically prepared for maximum speed. Panel gaps were filled with a putty-like substance and surfaces painted smooth, polished and waxed with increased tension in the flight controls. The guns were taken out and replaced with an 110USgal fuel tank to replace the wing tanks now used for engine water. Thus injected into the engine, water reduced the volume of air in the compressor section which increased the mass flow and provided added thrust. But only for short periods. The AAF provided six engines for use in the speed runs but these were also providing data which would aid improvements in overall performance for standard engines. Major Kenneth Chilstrom was assigned to trial runs.

Despite persistent attempts, Chilstrom could only reach 596mph (958.9km/hr) and this was bad news when, on 7 September Group Captain E M Donaldson flying a Gloster Meteor F.4 (EE549) again broke the world air speed record with a run at 615.78mph (990.8km/hr). Moreover, there was another contender with apparently better prospects. A Republic XP-84 was achieving runs above 600mph (965km/hr) and looking good for regaining the record from the British, the first time it would have held the all-out speed record for more than 20 years. Captain Albert Boyd was put in charge of getting things going at a more productive pace but the XP-84's J35, water-injected engine was unstable and under-developed. The record attempt was going to rest on the performance of the P-80A.

Now designated the XP-80R, the modified aircraft had the uprated Allison J33-A-17 engine. Two further attempts were made, on 2 and 4 October during which it appeared to have achieved record-breaking speeds, the average being the number taken as the contender. But scrutiny of the data showed that it had not and a third attempt on 5 October was abandoned. It was Johnson himself who discovered the reason: the modified, low-drag intakes were compromising the ram-air effect and not giving the engine optimum performance, as extrapolated from previous bench tests. Equipped with the more powerful, 4,600lb (20.46kN) Allison Model 400 (J33-A-23) engine, the XP-80R was given the appropriate nickname *Racey*. Weather kept the next series of record attempts at bay as Muroc flight activity paused for the winter months, a not unusual occurrence.

On 19 June 1947 all was ready, the weather was almost ideal, the aircraft had been polished to a near-mirror finish and the engine and intake alignment was optimised with the changes crafted by Johnson. Four high-speed runs were completed and when the results came in the average of all four was a record-breaking 623.74mph (1,003.6km/hr). It would not remain so for long. On 20 August, Commander Turner Caldwell snatched it for the US Navy with a record 640.663mph (1,031.049km/hr) in the Douglas D558-1 Skystreak research aircraft. It was exceeded five days later by Marine Corps pilot Major Marion Carl with a speed of 650.796mph (1,047.356km/hr) in the same aircraft. But the Skystreak was a pure research aircraft.

Immediately after the war and with independence looming, the Air Force was keen to show itself off and took three P-80s in a flight across the country from Burbank, California, to New York, piloted by Colonel William H Councill, Captain Martin L Smith and Captain John S Babel. Departing on 26 January 1946, they left the Army Air Base at Long Beach, California, on instruments due to local fog. Smith and Babel were flying on internal fuel and standard tip tanks with 150USgal each and planned a refuelling stop at Topeka, Kansas. Councill's aircraft had an extra-large tank on each wingtip bringing total fuel load to 1,145USgal, 400USgal more than the total fuel carried in a standard DC-3, raising gross weight to 16,900lb (7,665kg)! The post-flight recollections of Colonel Council are noteworthy because of the impact the flight had on the confidence with which the Air Force could expand the operating envelope for this aircraft and for jets in general:

> The flight as far as Kansas was very much routine for all of us. We levelled out at about 35,000ft (10,670m) using oxygen to supplement our pressurised cockpits. We all wore the regular leather summer flying jackets and were plenty warm. It is hard to convince yourself that you are flying the fastest plane of the Army Air Forces. The clatter of a trainer at 100 miles an hour (161km/hr) gives a greater sensation of speed than the quiet cockpit of a Shooting Star travelling almost six times as fast. Unless you keep your eye on the gauges all the time and believe your indicated air speed, that plane will tell you every time.
>
> There was no roar of a giant engine – only a quiet swishing sound which reminded me of coasting downhill in a free-wheeling Packard. The super General Electric turbojet was

The clean lines of the P-80 design was a hallmark of the Lockheed Shooting Star, which was created in the company's Skunk Works specifically set up to develop the P-38 and then this highly secret jet fighter. (USAF)

developing up to 4,000 pounds of thrust (17.79kPh) behind my back, but I could hardly hear it. I was at sustained cruising speed nearly all the way to save on fuel consumption. There was no vibration at all, I felt smooth, surging power whenever I advanced the singe throttle lever slightly. But there was never the quick acceleration that snaps your head back with its forward thrust.

At first I could not believe the old familiar checkpoints on the Great Circle Course as I noted them on the flight plan. My knee pad recorded: 870 miles (1,400km) to La Junta, Colorado in 1 hr 38 min; 1,020 miles (1,641km) to Garden City, Kansas, in 1 hr 55 min; 1,190 miles (1,915km) to Salina, Kansas, in 2 hrs nine minutes; 1,350 miles (2,172km) to St Joseph, Missouri, in 2 hrs 28 minutes; 1,475 miles (2,373km) to Kirksville, Missouri, in 2 hrs 38.5 minutes; 1,700 miles (2,735km) to Chanute Field, Illinois, in 3 hrs two minutes; 2,050 miles (3,298km) to Akron, Oklahoma, in 3 hrs 34 minutes; and 2,470 miles (3,974km) to La Guardia Field, New York, in 4 hrs 13 minutes 26 seconds at an average speed of 584.82mph (940.97km/hr) from coast to coast.

Captains Smith and Babel landed at Topeka for what was probably the fastest refuelling job on record. Fourteen Lockheed field service experts were ready with four fuel trucks and a crew of ground men to meet and service the planes from any angle of approach. They were ready to change an engine if necessary in less than 18 minutes. Completely serviced, Captain Babel was in the air again four minutes after his wheels had touched the ground. Captain Smith, who had been bothered with a landing wheel door which wouldn't quite close, was delayed an extra two minutes while the special crew worked on it.

Just after I jettisoned my extra-large fuel tanks, I passed Captain Smith climbing out of Topeka. In the vicinity of St Joseph, Missouri, I moved up to 41,000ft (12,497m). The perfect weather held out until Akron. But from there on, I was on instruments most of the way, and hit some turbulence when crossing the Alleghenies. In spite of that, I made my highest air speed on that leg when I approached the rated altitude. I started my let down from 41,000ft (12,497m) at Sunbury, Pennsylvania, and buzzed La Guardia at 2,000ft (610m). My indicator registered 615mph (989km/hr) across the field. I still had left 120 gallons of kerosene.

Hitching a Lift

While overall the P-80 acquitted itself well and displayed good performance for its size and engine power, there was concern about its range and the ability to support requirements. As noted in the Appendix, optional ideas had been presented for carrying fighters inside future bombers until they were needed for defence. Another idea was to tow the fighter behind the bomber into denied airspace where it could start its engine and be released for free flight, engaging in combat with enemy aircraft. The fighter could then reconnect to the bomber and shut down its engine for a tow back to base. One P-80A (44-84995) was assigned to this test project at Wright Field. The aircraft was fitted with a special towing bar in the nose for carrying electrical power to the fighter which could be engaged or released by the fighter pilot.

A modified B-29A (42-93921) was assigned to these tests and on 23 September 1947 Lieutenant Colonel Pat Fleming rendezvoused with the bomber and attempted to engage with the tow line but turbulence interfered and only after several attempts was the connection made. For 10 minutes the two aircraft flew together but when an attempt was made to disconnect, the bar would not let go of the line until Fleming flew underneath the bomber and nudged

A P-80 (44-85155) of the 412th FG which was modified later into an RF-80A-15-10. (USAF)

forward so that the bow wave from the fuselage of the B-29 bent the bar causing it to snap. Both aircraft landed safely but it was clear that the concept was flawed, unsafe and impractical. The P-80A was reconfigured for service use and returned to its operational deployment.

Several other experimental tests were conducted for applications which had been pioneered by the *Luftwaffe* during the Second World War and which had been observed during combat operations over occupied Europe. One of those was the *Schräge Musik*, a colloquial German phrase for 'jazz music' in which fighters carried upward-firing guns to attack a bomber from underneath in its most vulnerable and least protected place. This adaptation was introduced by German fighter units when the general defensive arrangement of the B-17 and the B-24 had been studied, identifying the earlier slash-attack conducted at high speed and at an angle to the bomber's flight path as dangerous.

One P-80A (44-85044) was taken off the line and modified to have upward-firing machine guns in the nose with an internal articulated mount allowing an elevation of up to 90 degrees from the aircraft's centreline. When the guns were fired the effect was near catastrophic with predictable consequences as the aircraft pitched and bucked like a demented horse preventing any degree of accuracy as the bullets flailed around without any precision as to an intended target. One aircraft (44-85116) was fitted with jettisonable 5-in (12.7cm) rockets in place of the wingtip tanks and further tests were made with a rocket launcher in the nose in place of the guns. Another aircraft (44-85354) was fitted with four 20mm cannon in lieu of the six machine guns but it was not successful.

In the never-ending search for speed, ramjet propulsion was a plausible means of supplementing the turbojet engine and another P-80A (44-85214) was fitted with two Marquardt 30-inch (76.2cm) wingtip ramjets in place of the tip tanks while another (44-85042) carried two Marquardt 10-inch (127cm) tip ramjets. First flown on 12 March 1947 to good effect, they operated as the sole forms of propulsion on 17 June 1948. In all, 100 flights were made, most by Lockheed test pilot Herman R Salmon but the fuel consumption for the ramjets was far too high to warrant operational deployment.

Begun by a Lockheed proposal for a more advanced version initially known as the P-80Z, the next variant, the P-80B would have the Allison J33-A-17 engine with space for the water-alcohol injection tanks obtained at the cost of internal fuel capacity, reduced from 470USgal to 425USgal, a modification installed on the prototype, the ninth P-80A (44-85200) and redesignated as the XP-80B following the variant's approval in April 1945. Some reports and several books have claimed that the P-80B had a thinner wing and a thicker skin but that is not so. The wing remained the same on all production aircraft. But it did have stronger nose bulkheads to support six .50-in machine guns, with a cockpit canopy defrosting kit and an improved cooling system.

The P-80B was the first US combat aircraft to have an ejection seat, designed and built by Lockheed, and there was also provision for attaching JATO (jet assisted take-off) rockets to assist take-off runs which, for jet aircraft, could be far greater than with propeller-driven types. The only external difference was the relocation of the pitot-tube from the nose to the fin. The darker nose fairing incorporated a loop antenna for the Bendix AN/ARN-6 radio compass, with an automatic direction-finding set covering 100kHz to 455.9kHz in four bands. The XP-50B was the aircraft redefined as the XP-80R for the world speed record attempts noted above.

The letter contract for the P-80B was awarded in December 1946 with an order for 60 aircraft, raised to 140 on 31 January 1947, of which 60 were to have gone to the ANG but that was reduced to 54 when the budget cuts kicked in. Eventually, the Air Force would receive 240 P-80Bs by March 1948 when production ended, redesignated F-80B from June 1948 when the nomenclature changed. One aircraft (45-8484) was significantly modified in 1953 to conduct tests with the Bell GAM-63 missile, gaining a longer, pointed nose, with tip tanks carrying the guidance system and with new vertical control surfaces above and below the wings at mid-span.

The final variant, the P-80C, for which the signed order did not appear until 2 February 1948, carried very few changes but is most notably defined for having two different and more powerful engines: the first 188 were fitted with the 4,600lb (20.46kN) thrust Allison J33-A-23 while the remaining 561 produced had the 5,200lb (23.13kN) thrust J33-A-35 engines. The P-80C was 36mph (58km/hr) faster than the P-80A and had a climb rate of 6,870ft/min (2,094m/min) versus 4,580ft/min (1,396m/min) for the P-80A. The normal range was much improved: 825miles (1,327km) for the

This F-80C-10-LO (49-696) was assigned to the 35th FBS, 8th Fighter-Bomber Group at Itazuke AB, Japan. It would later fly combat missions during the Korean War, be loaned to the Uruguayan Air Force in 1958 and returned to the United States where it resides today in the National Museum of the US Air Force and bears the markings of the 8th FBG of 1950. (NMUSAF)

P-80C versus 780miles (1,255km) for the P-80A. The first P-80C (47-171) was built almost entirely of magnesium and made its first flight on 30 April 1948.

This variant was subject to several contractual changes, the Air Force eventually receiving 670 against a projected 798 ordered. The last 128 were converted into TF-80C types which became the first T-33As, redesignated as such on 5 May 1949. The way the two-seat trainer came about is a lesson in company commitment and a personal resolve to provide a solution to a potentially intractable problem. As noted previously, jet aircraft were notoriously difficult to fly for pilots transitioning straight from propeller-driven aircraft. Acceleration was slow during take-off and the engine was frequently slow to respond to throttle commands; some aircraft in this period had 'gate-limiters' restricting the authority of the throttle lever. A two-seat trainer was insurance against premature disaster.

Two to Tango

Before the first flight of the XP-80, Lockheed's vice-president for military relations, Mac V F Short pushed for a trainer to lessen the risk of a pilot killing himself and to reduce the attrition rate in airframes. Uninterested at first, the Air Force became alarmed by the number of aircraft lost in accidents and in 1947 accepted the need for a trainer adapted from the basic P-80 design. Putting company money into developing a bespoke variant for that purpose, the Model 880 was designed by a team led by Don Palmer and an airframe was assigned to modify the P-80C into a TF-80C (48-356) by adding an instructor's seat behind the existing cockpit space.

Palmer cut the fuselage and inserted a 38.5in (98cm) plug forward of the wing leading-edge and adding a 12-inch (30.5cm) piece aft, reducing the fuselage fuel tank capacity from 207USgal to 95USgal. To compensate, the self-sealing wing tanks were replaced with flexible nylon cells restoring capacity to 353USgal, compared to 425USgal for the standard fighter variant. A single-piece clear canopy enveloped both fore and aft ejection seat positions and weight was saved by removing all but two of the two .50-in guns. Tony LeVier took the prototype for its first flight on 22 March 1948.

It was a winner. The type was taken on a tour of Air Force facilities and additional orders quickly resulted. Including foreign production, a total of 5,691 were built and the T-33 remained the prime Air Force trainer for more than 10 years. Additional variants brought production total to 6,557, the last delivered in 1959. Work to develop the TF-33 gave Lockheed the head-start to fast-track development of the F-94 two-seat, all-weather fighter, which we will cover later and in Volume 4, where more complete details of the photographic reconnaissance variants, maximised for operational duty in the Korean War, can be found.

Long before that conflict, following the initial modification to the second YP-80A (44-83024) to contain cameras in the nose, another P-80A (44-85201) was more comprehensively modified as a precursor to a production reconnaissance variant. This aircraft was given a hinged nose to afford better access to the cameras. The production version was an RF-80A, the first (44-85383) of 38 P-80A aircraft converted on the assembly line. It was delivered to the 12th PRS at March AFB in August 1946 but it was written off at Palm Beach, California, on 1 October 1947 in an accident from which the pilot survived.

A new line of 114 reconnaissance aircraft was produced with the first of those (45-8364) designated FP-80A, and RF-80A from June 1948. These had the same hinged nose and were powered by a 3,850lb (17.12kN) thrust J33-GE-11 turbojet and carried a K-17 aerial camera equipped with a 6-inch (15cm) lens and two K-22 cameras with 24-inch (61cm) lenses. In 1953, one of these aircraft would be modified to carry a 5,400lb (24kN) thrust J33-A-35. A further modification was made in 1951 when 70 standard F-80As were brought up to near-F-80C standard and given the J33-A-35 engine together with further improvement to the camera complement contained within a modified nose and redesignated RF-80C.

There might have been one further variant of the Shooting Star through Lockheed's Model 680-33-07 which could have been designated F-80D, had it not been cancelled as unnecessary in the light of enhanced development with other and more capable fighters emerging from the stable of first-generation jets. When proposed in June 1948 it would have had improved electronics and some modifications to the flight systems, adopting new equipment for better flight operations and several cockpit features from the T-33. Lockheed proposed that it have the J33-A-29 turbojet with afterburner, delivering a wet thrust of 8,200lb (36.4kN).

In a concerted effort to develop the Shooting Star into an aerodynamically more refined aircraft, in May 1948 Lockheed proposed its Model L-181, or P-80E, which would have had swept wings and tail. Responding to the capabilities of the Republic F-84 and the North American F-86, Lockheed sought to maintain its grip on the fighter market with this redesigned version. It would be a development on the P-80C and would have had a thinner wing and tailplane swept at 35 degrees. Powered by an Allison J33-A-27 afterburning turbojet, an engine developed from the US Navy's J33-A-16A, the P-80E was calculated to have a maximum speed of 662mph (1,065km/hr) with a combat range of 1,760 miles (2,832km).

Operational deployment of the P-80 began with the 55th FG at Geibelstadt, Germany, in 1946, remaining there until early 1948. When the Russians began the Berlin blockade in June 1948 a single squadron of the 56th FG made the first west-east transatlantic crossing with this type in the July, remaining in country for 45 days whereupon they were replaced by fresh P-80s with the 36th FG at Fürstenfeldbruck near Munich. To increase USAFE's tactical air strength, in July 1948 75 F-80s were transferred to the 36th FG, a move that considerably increased USAFE's tactical airpower, but also was considered as having great psychological value.

Table 2: Lockheed P/F-80 Shooting Star Specifications

	XP-80	P-80A	F-80B	F-80C
Span	37ft/11.27m	38.83ft/11.83m	39ft/11.89m	38.75ft/11.81m
Length	32.83ft/10.00m	34.5ft/10.51m	34.5ft/10.51m	34.41ft/10.49m
Height	10.25ft/3.12m	11.33ft/3.45m	11.33ft/3.45m	11.25ft/3.42m
Empty weight	6,287lb/2,852kg	7,920lb/3,593kg	8,176lb/3,709kg	8,420lb/3,819kg
Gross weight	8,620lb/3,910kg	11,700lb/5,307kg	12,200lb/5,534kg	12,200lb/5,534kg
Max speed	502mph/808kph	492mph/792kph	577mph/929kph	543mph/874kph
Ceiling	41,000ft/12,497m	45,000ft/13,716m	45,500ft/13,868m	46,800ft/14,265m
Range	1,000mls/1,609km	780mls/1,255km	790mls/1,271km	825mls/1,328km

US AIR POWER 1945–1990 VOLUME 1: US FIGHTERS AND FIGHTER-BOMBERS 1945–1949

The North American P-51H Mustang was the final single-engined production variant of the legendary Mustang family. Manufactured from 1945 onwards, it received a more powerful Rolls-Royce Merlin engine, improved aerodynamics, and increased speed. This P-51H served with the 62nd Fighter Squadron, 56th Fighter Group, home-based at Selfridge Field, Harrison Township, Michigan, in 1947. (Artwork by Jean-Marie Guillou)

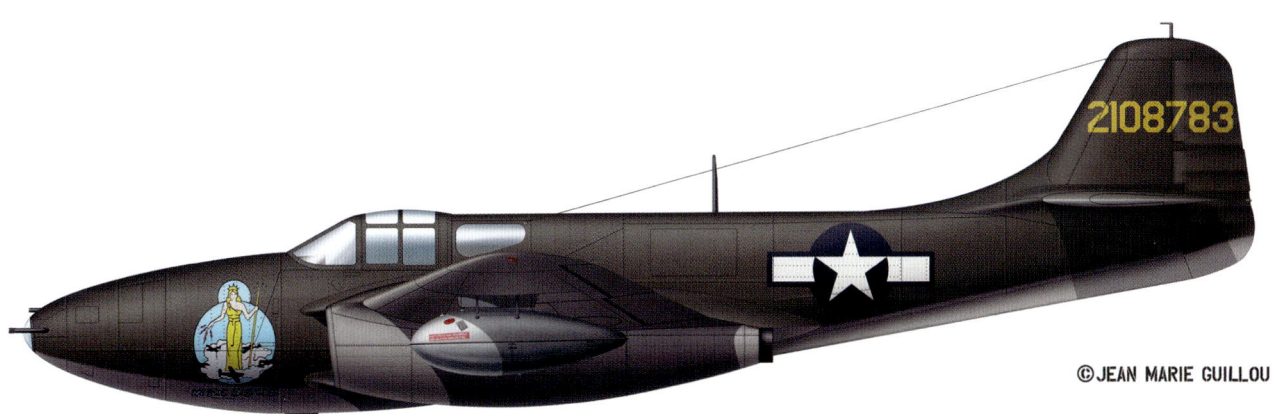

The Bell P-59A was the first operational jet used by the United States Army Air Force. Developed in 1944–1945, it featured a unique blend of British and American design influences. The United States Army Air Forces (USAAF) placed an order for 100, but when the General Electric J31 engine proved to be underperforming, this contract was cancelled and the type relegated to training duties. Eventually, only 20 P-59As were completed, their deliveries taking place in the autumn of 1944. This P-59A was operated by the 412th Fighter Group, home-based at Muroc Army Airfield, California, in 1945. The aircraft was nicknamed 'Mystic Mistress'. (Artwork by Jean-Marie Guillou)

In addition to 20 P-59As, 30 P-59Bs were also constructed (serial numbers were 44-22629 to 44-22658), these had an extra fuel tank in their outer wing panels. Most served with the 412th Fighter Group where they were used to familiarise USAAF pilots with the handling and performance characteristics of jet aircraft. Three, including this example, were handed over to the US Navy, which test-flew them at the Naval Air Test Center (NATC) at NAS Patuxent River. Although receiving the designation YF2L-1, they quickly proved unsuitable for carrier operations and were operated only for a few months. (Artwork by Jean-Marie Guillou)

The Bell P-80A was a major improvement over any jets available in the USA by 1945. Its streamlined design and the reliable and relatively powerful General Electric I-40 engine (based on a donated British Goblin) enabled it to see a little action during the last few weeks of the Second World War and it would go on to see more during the Korean War, where it demonstrated its effectiveness as a ground-attack aircraft. This P-80A (serial number 44-85275) was assigned to Lieutenant Colonel William D Ritchie, commanding officer of the 61st Fighter Squadron, 56th Fighter Group, home-based at Selfridge AFB. (Artwork by Jean-Marie Guillou)

The North American P-82 Twin Mustang was the last US-made piston-engined fighter to enter series production. Based on the design of the P-51, it was originally envisaged as a long-range escort fighter for Boeing B-29 Superfortress bombers. The war ended before it became operational, and subsequently it entered service as a replacement for the Northrop P-61 Black Widow, as an all-weather and night interceptor. This P-82G (serial number 46-357) was flown by captains Ralph D. Mulhollen and Arild C Nielsen, from the 68th Fighter-Interceptor Squadron, 6160th Air Bases Wing, from Itazuke in Japan, as of June 1950. (Artwork by Jean-Marie Guillou)

Designed as a day fighter and first flown in 1946, the Republic F-84 Thunderjet was initially plagued by structural- and engine-related problems. Indeed, by 1948, it was close to cancellation when the F-84D model matured as its definitive form. Following many refinements, the F-84E, followed by the ultimate F-84G, entered service in 1950, just in time to become the USAF's primary strike aircraft during the Korean War. This F-84E was assigned to the 36th Fighter Bomber Group, home-based at Fürstenfeldbruck in the early 1950s. Yellow wingtip tanks denoted it as assigned to the 53rd Fighter Bomber Squadron. Notably, the cockpit canopy was that of an F-84G. (Artwork by Jean-Marie Guillou)

Powered by the General Electric J47-GE-7 engine, the F-86A quickly turned into an iconic early jet fighter, known not only for its swept wing design, but exceptional manoeuvrability. Combined with its top speed of over 670mph (1,078km/h) this enabled it to play a crucial role as an air superiority fighter capable of countering the slightly superior Soviet MiG-15s. This was an F-86A of the 94th Fighter Squadron, 1st Fighter Group – the first unit to receive Sabres. (Artwork by Jean-Marie Guillou)

The F-89 Scorpion was designed to a 1945 requirement for an all-weather fighter with designs provided by several US manufacturers and the initial concept for a piston-engine type changed to incorporate two jets. Northrop received the contract to produce the F-89, although that was contested by losing contenders with the first flight taking place on 16 August 1948. The aircraft shown here is one of the 11 F-89A accepted by the Air Force with 49-2435 redesignated an NF-89 operated by the Proving Ground Command Center, Eglin AFB, Florida. (Artwork by Goran Sudar)

The F-89A, F-89B, and F-89C were the initial production models of the Scorpion: a big, all-weather interceptor with a fascinating design. The A model entered service in 1951, and featured equipment including guns and rudimentary electronic systems only. Because they were primarily tasked with air defence duties, and the Air National Guard played a crucial role in augmenting active-duty forces during the early stages of the Cold War, F-89As were assigned to such assets as the 120th Fighter-Interceptor Wing of the Montana Air National Guard, illustrated here. (Artwork by Goran Sudar)

The primary task of the F-89 was intercepting Soviet heavy bombers. The original armament configuration envisaged six 15mm or 20mm guns, which were soon considered insufficient. Therefore, the second specification required the installation of six guns: two forward and four aft, each capable of 15 degrees of movement from the aircraft's longitudinal axis. Meanwhile, the Martin Corporation had designed the D-1 fire-control system for the still-born Curtiss F-87 project; this included a turret-like nose that could be rotated through 360° around the longitudinal axis. The section containing four 20mm guns could be elevated to 105°, offering a huge field of fire. Eventually, the D-1 was installed and flight tested on this F-89A (serial number 49-2434). (Artwork by Goran Sudar)

Developed from the RT-33 Shooting Star reconnaissance aircraft, the F-94 had a stretched fuselage with Hughes E-5 fire-control system in the top section of the nose, and guns below it, to serve as an interim all-weather interceptor. The rear fuselage was stretched and widened to make space for the more powerful Pratt & Whitney J48 engine for the C and D variants, which offered excellent acceleration, and good manoeuvrability and rate of climb. This F-94B-1-LO, serial number 50-0888, was operated by the 61st Fighter-Interceptor Squadron, which converted to F-94s in 1950 and flew them until 1957. (Artwork by Goran Sudar)

The F-94 saw extensive service with the Air Defense Command of the US Air Force, where between 1950 and 1958 it served with a total of 26 squadrons. Three squadrons also served in the Far East Air Force, the Alaskan Air Command and the Northeast Air Command. It played a significant role in helping develop and further improve tactical methods. This F-94B-1-LO serial number 50-829, was operated by the 319th Fighter-Interceptor Squadron, forward deployed at Suwon AB, in the Republic of South Korea, in March 1951, and then at Misawa AFB, in Japan, in 1952, where one was lost while pursuing an unknown aircraft by night. (Artwork by Goran Sudar)

Although the USAF was lukewarm about purchasing an upgraded variant, the F-94C was modified extensively enough to be given the designation F-97. It included a completely new, much thinner wing, along with swept tail surfaces, the Pratt & Whitney J48 engine (a licence version of the Rolls-Royce Tay), and an upgraded E-5 weapons system including an AN/APG-40 radar. The guns were removed and replaced by all-rocket armament consisting of four groups of six rockets installed in a ring around the nose. The only variant officially named Starfire, 387 were manufactured. (Artwork by Goran Sudar)

Upon its introduction in 1952, the F-94C displayed poor performance but after 10 test aircraft flew for data-gathering, changes and improvements were made although engines continued to be troublesome. This F-94C-1-10 (50-1054) was delivered to the 60th FIS in 1953 before serving with the 437th FTS (564th ANG) later that year. It was written off at Otis AFB, Massachusetts, and displayed later at Monument Beach, Massachusetts. (Artwork by Goran Sudar)

The Consolidated Vultee XP-81 was a single-seat, long-range escort fighter designed to be powered by both turbojet- and turboprop engines. Two protypes were ordered in February 1944 and equipped with a General Electric TG-100 turboprop – meant to be used for cruise flight – and a General Electric J33 turbojet, to be used for high-speed flight. Both examples suffered due to development problems, causing their reengining with a V-1650-7 engine of the P-51D. Although showing good handling characteristics, and the USAAF having requested 13 pre-production aircraft, the order was cancelled when Japan capitulated on 2 September 1945. Flight testing was continued until 1947, when both XP-81s were reduced to targets on a bombing range. (Artwork by Goran Sudar)

Planned to become an escort fighter, the XP-83 was also to correct the P-59's problems with the low fuel load and short range. While based on the P-59 design, it had a pressurised cockpit. However, the performance in terms of the lack of power and directional instability, was disappointing, especially in comparison to the P-80, and the project was cancelled. The first prototype thus ended as a testbed for ramjet engines, and crashed in 1946, while the second was flown in October 1946, but then scrapped only a few months later. (Artwork by Goran Sudar)

The Convair XF-92 was designed as a point defence interceptor with delta wing, capable of reaching speeds of 700mph (1,100km/h) at an altitude of 50,000ft (15,000m) in four minutes from take-off. The design was frozen in 1946 and accepted for development, but Consolidated Vultee was still constructing the first prototype when the company was bought by North American in the summer of 1947, and the work moved to Convair in San Diego. The XF-92A was flown for the first time in June 1948, but before long was relegated to experimental purposes related to the development of delta-shaped wings. (Artwork by Goran Sudar)

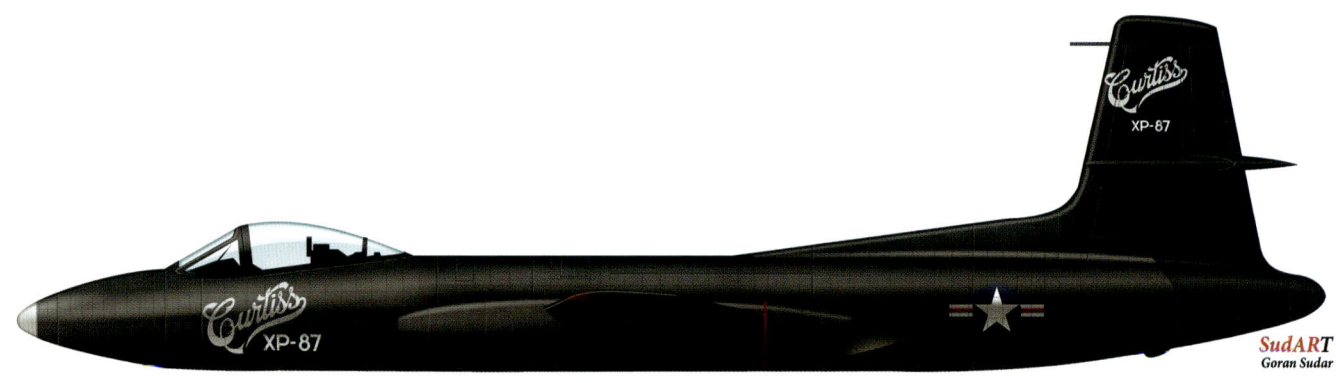

The Curtiss-Wright XP-87 Blackhawk was designed as an all-weather jet-powered interceptor. Powered by a total of four ill-fated Westinghouse XJ34 turbojets (which were to spoil a number of US fighter projects), it was first flown on 5 March 1948, but promptly proved slower than expected, even if 'otherwise acceptable'. The USAF placed an order for 57 F-87A interceptors and 30 RF-87A reconnaissance fighters but before the J34s could be replaced by General Electric J47s, lost interest due to the appearance of the Northrop F-89 and cancelled the project on 10 October 1948. (Artwork by Goran Sudar)

The McDonnell XF-85 Goblin came into being during the Second World War in response to the requirement for a 'parasite fighter' for the giant Convair B-36 bomber: the idea was for the bombers to deploy them as a means of self-defence against enemy interceptors. Therefore, the jet had to be very small, to fit – at least partially – within the bomb bay. The prototypes were constructed and flight testing began only in 1948 but proved promising enough for the project to be continued. It was only once it became clear that the XF-85's performance was poorer than that of the competition and there were difficulties with docking, that the project was cancelled. The USAF continued examining the concept of parasite fighter until the Boeing B-47 demonstrated performance that made them unnecessary. (Artwork by Goran Sudar)

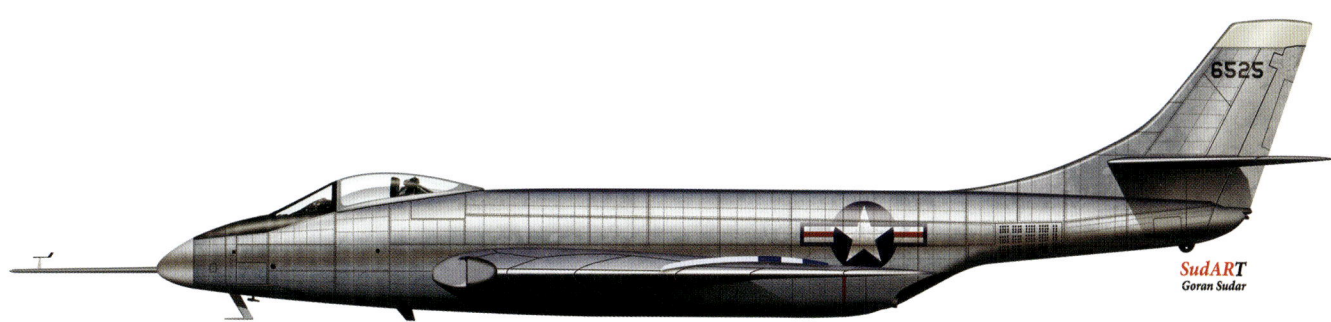

The first McDonnell XF-88 was based on a requirement for a long-range, twin-engined fighter jet with swept wings, issued by the USAAF in 1946. The first XF-88 was powered by non-afterburning J34-13 engines – which doomed it to remain underpowered, although flight testing showed adequate handling and the required endurance. The first prototype was subsequently equipped with an Allison XT-35-A-5 turboprop for testing purposes: as the XF-88B, it became the first propeller-powered aircraft to break the sound barrier. (Artwork by Goran Sudar)

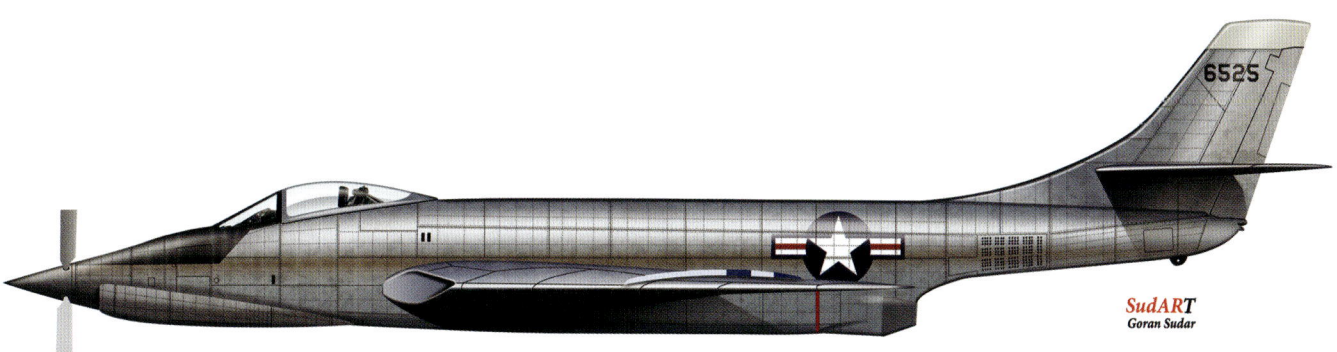

When the first XP-88 prototype proved underpowered, the decision was taken to equip the second with J34-22 engines that had primitive afterburners. Although this shortened the range – because of higher fuel consumption – a similar modification was also undertaken on the first XF-88. Eventually, the USAF picked this type over the Lockheed XF-90 and North American YF-93 and planned to place an order for a Westinghouse J46-powered variant. However, combat experience from Korea and the flight performance of the B-47 proved that penetration fighters were unnecessary and the project was cancelled. Nevertheless, McDonnell continued work on two XP-88s and their revised design eventually became the F-101 Voodoo. (Artwork by Goran Sudar)

The Republic XF-91 Thunderceptor was another of several mixed-propulsion projects for interceptor aircraft during the late 1940s. It was planned to use a jet engine for cruise speed, and a cluster of four small rocket engines for climb and combat. Although two prototypes were constructed – the first equipped with radar and the second with the butterfly fin – the combination of rapid development of jet engines, short range (the endurance of the Thunderceptor was limited to some 25 minutes), and the design of their fuselages rendered them obsolete. (Artwork by Goran Sudar)

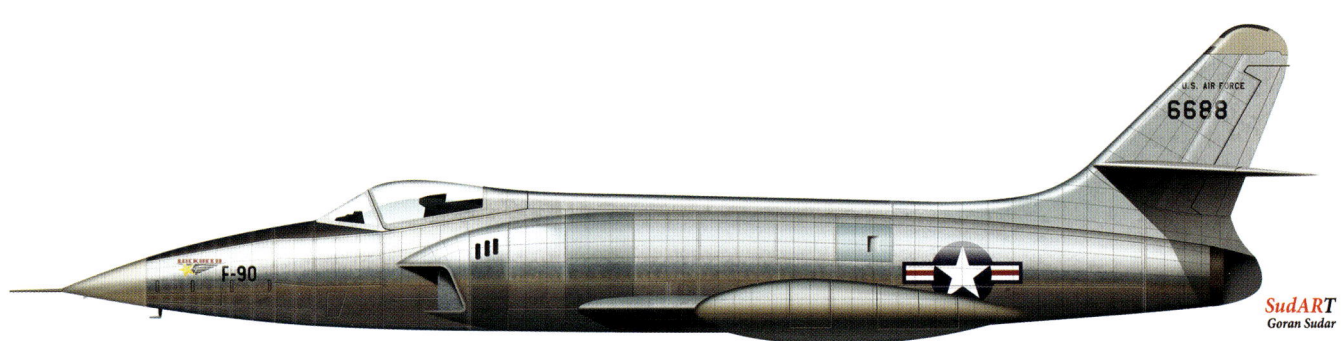

The Lockheed XF-90 was another contender for the penetration fighter project. Developed from the design of the successful P-80, the two prototypes had swept wings and two engines, but the Westinghouse J34-EW-11s proved woefully insufficient for the task, although the XF-90 thus became the first USAF jet equipped with afterburners. Including an unusual vertical stabiliser – which could be moved fore and aft for adjustment – the XF-90 was to include six 20mm guns. The first prototype (only two were ever built) broke the sound barrier (even if only in a dive), but Lockheed's contender came out second after the XF-88, before the entire contest was cancelled. (Artwork by Goran Sudar)

The YF-93 was North American's late entry for the penetration fighter contest. Although based on the F-86, it was a radically different aircraft with a much higher take-off weight, wider fuselage, larger wing area, intakes submerged into the fuselage underneath the cockpit, and the more powerful Pratt & Whitney J48 engine. Originally designated the F-86C, when the USAF placed its order for two prototypes in December 1947 they were redesignated as the YF-93A. Six months later, an order for 118 aircraft was placed, but the entire contest was cancelled before any of the production aircraft could be completed. The two prototypes (48-317 and 48-318) were constructed but they ended serving with the National Advisory Committee for Aeronautics, where they had conventional intakes instead. (Artwork by Goran Sudar)

In the United States, aircraft went to the 4th FG at Langley AFB, Virginia, the 81st FG at Kirtland AFB, New Mexico, the 57th FG at Elmendorf AFB, Alaska, together with some squadrons of Air Defense Command. The 1st and 56th FGs with Strategic Air Command also received their Shooting Stars in 1948.

In 1949 the first F-80s sent to Japan equipped the 51st FG and by the end of the year the aircraft was equipping units in the Far East Air Force (FEAF) and would be in theatre for the start of the Korean War on 25 June 1950, a period covered in Volume 4 where its operational history is presented. In all, the Air Force received 1,731 F-80s of which the greatest production run was the 670 F-80Cs followed by the 525 F-80As.

North American P-82 Twin Mustang; First Flight: 15 June 1945

During the last two years of the Second World War, with the Eighth AF in England participating in a combined bomber offensive with the RAF, protecting the daylight bombers was an urgent priority. On the night of 17 August 1943 and again on 14 October, in raids on the Schweinfurt ball-bearing factories, 120 B-17s (25 percent of the main force) were shot down with the loss of 1,200 airmen killed or captured. Earlier, the Americans had thought that once they had crossed the German air-defence fighter-belt laid out across north-western continental Europe as the Kammhuber-line they would receive little opposition. That had been a serious error and the need for bomber escort to and from the target became a necessity and so it was also judged to be in the Pacific war.

The search for a long-range escort fighter to protect the B-29 force flying from bases in the Solomon Islands to targets in Japan, a distance of 2,000 miles (3,200km), was urgent. The range requirement was far in excess of that for a similar bomber escort role in the European air war, which from 1944 was being ably filled with the P-51D Mustang, but development of a new aircraft for the Pacific theatre would take too long. On 7 January 1944, North American presented a bold design, consisting of two lengthened, lightweight P-51 fuselage assemblies similar to the P-51H, joined together by a separate wing section, the fuselage tails being connected by a rectangular section.

The connecting wing section would support six .50-in M2 machine guns and the two cockpits would have dual controls, two pilots being essential for the 12-hr endurance capability so that one could rest at appropriate times. Under the company model number of NAA-120, the Air Force immediately grasped the advantage and on 8 February awarded a contract for two XP-82 prototypes to be powered by the Packard Rolls-Royce V-1650 carried over from production Merlin engines. The entire configuration was vaguely similar to the proposed Messerschmitt Bf 109 Zwilling, which was never developed.

The first prototype XP-82 (44-83886) rolled out from NAA's Inglewood plant on 25 May 1945, by which date the war in Europe was over. Prior to this the AAF had ordered 500 production P-82s but when the Japanese surrendered it reduced this to 270, a type nevertheless which was felt crucial to the long-range bomber force heralded as the core of America's post-war airborne deterrent. The first flight was conducted by J E Barton and in subsequent tests it proved its worth, delivering a top speed of 468mph (753kph), exceeding that of the P-51D by 31mph (50kph). The single XP-82A (44-83888) was powered by the Allison V-1710 engine. The 10 production P-82Bs had the same Allison engine as the two prototypes and first flew on 19 October 1945, a type model used primarily for training pilots for the later operational variants.

Connecting two P-51 fighter fuselage units by a wing intersection and a connecting horizontal tail, the P/F-82 Twin Mustang had enviable performance. (USAF)

F-82 production facilities at North American Aviation in 1948, deliveries compromised by sluggish engine production. (NAA)

First flown on 17 February 1947, the F-82E followed the C, which had first flown on 27 March 1946, and the D, taking to the air two days later, both with radar scanners in pods attached to the wing intersection. Effectively a development of the XP-82A, the E variant had the more powerful Allison V-1710 engines, their adoption being only after successful operation powering the Curtiss P-40 and the Lockheed P-38 had demonstrated that this all-American engine could be substituted for the V-1610, which still had rights payable to Rolls-Royce. But the V-1710 was never as reliable or as efficient as the V-1610 and was dubbed the 'Allison time bomb'! But the V-1710 was powerful, with a rating of 2,250hp (1,677kw) driving 10.9ft (3.3m), fully feathering contra-rotating propellers.

The production contract for the Twin Mustang redefined the role by converting 150 to a night-fighter role based on the C and D variants. The F-82E was similar to the P-82B in essential respects but delivery was hampered by faltering engine production and technical issues with superchargers, spark plugs which had to be changed after every flight, oil leaks and surging. Only one F-82E had been delivered by the end of November 1947. North American had a build-up of flightless airframes awaiting their engines and hired space at a Vultee plant in Downey, California to accommodate them. The last of 96 airframes was completed in April 1948 but the final delivery of this variant only reached the Air Force in April 1949.

Most F-82Es went to the 27th Fighter-Escort Group with Strategic Air Command, showing 81 on strength from May 1948 and in 1949, where they were assigned long-range escort duty with the B-29s and the B-36s, many demonstration flights taking them to Panama and Puerto Rico. But their time was running out as inflight refuelling gave jet fighters the range to escort the bombers and by 1950 SAC had dispensed with their Twin Mustangs.

Flight trials against SAC bombers found them vulnerable to P-61 Black Widow night fighters, prompting development of interceptor F-82F and G variants, equipped with the AN/APG-18 and the SCR 720C18, respectively, in a bulbous housing on the wing intersection. This F-82F (46-415) served with the 2nd F(AW)S. (USAF)

A final application found the Twin Mustang conducting an all-weather interceptor role through the 92 F-82F, 45 F-82G and 14 F-82H variants. Making its first flight on 11 March 1948, the F-82F differed from the F-82E only in specialised equipment for the role, including the AN/APG-28 tracking radar in an enlarged pod mounted to the underwing centre section as had been trialled on the F-82D. For this role, the dual controls were removed from one cockpit with a radar operator replacing the co-pilot. It also carried glide path receiver, absolute altimeter, tail warning radar, localiser receiver, marker beacon, an AN/APN-19 radar beacon and IFF (identification friend or foe) equipment. This raised the gross weight to 22,080lb (10,015kg) with two 310USgal drop tanks but little compromise on performance.

The F-82F went to US Air Defense Command to replace the F-61 Black Widow at the 52nd F(AW)G at Mitchell AFB, New York from July 1948 and to the 325th F(AW)G at Moses Lake AFB, Washington, and the 449th F(AW)S at Ladd AFB, Alaska, by the end of October.

With a first flight on 8 December 1947, several months before the F-82F, the F-82G was virtually identical to its contemporary and operated with the 347th F(AW)G in the Far East, again replacing the F-61 at Okinawa, Itazuke and Yokota. Operations conducted during the Korean War are recorded in Volume 4.

The final variants were modified for cold-weather operation and given the designation F-82H, also including nine F-82F and five F-82G airframes with de-icing equipment and boots together with electric heaters on the propeller blades. The first flight of an H variant took place on 15 February 1949 with almost all conversions serving with the 449th F(AW)S at Ladd AFB as replacements for the F and G variants which were not weather-adapted. These would fly photo-reconnaissance missions over the Bering Strait using hand-held cameras since the radar pod equipment occupied space otherwise allotted to special camera pods. They would be replaced by F-94B Starfire interceptors but the last F-82H was not retired until June 1953.

On 27 February 1947 this F-82B (44-65168), named *Betty Joe* after one of the pilots, flew 5,051 miles (8,127km) from Hawaii to New York City in 14 hours and 33 minutes, a world record for a piston-engine fighter. It later served with the NACA's Lewis Research Center for tests with an underwing ramjet engine and bearing the code EFQ. (NACA)

Another view of the ramjet engine tested by the NACA for potential application as a propulsion boost for high-speed interception. (NACA)

The story of the F-82 Twin Mustang might have ended right there, a legacy programme from a fading age of propeller-driven fighters hanging on through secondary applications for a stop-gap function until replaced by jet-powered fighters and interceptors. But on 28 February 1947, the Twin Mustang sealed its place in aviation history, securing a world endurance record for piston-engine aircraft which remains unsurpassed to this day. Piloting the ninth production F-82B, Commander Robert E Thacker and Lieutenant John M Ard flew from Hickam Field, Hawaii, to LaGuardia Field, New York, a total distance of 4,968 miles (7,993km) in 14 hours 31 minutes 50 seconds, nonstop and without inflight refuelling. Supplementary fuel tanks were attached for a take-off load of 2,215USgal flying at an average speed of 342mph (550km/hr).

Table 3: North American P-82 Twin Mustang Specifications

	XP-82	P-82B	P-82E	P-82F
Span	51.25ft/15.62m	51.25ft/15.62m	51.25ft/15.62m	51.25ft/15.62m
Length	39.08ft/11.91m	39.08ft/11.91m	39.08ft/11.91m	42.16ft/12.85m
Height	13.83ft/4.21m	13.83ft/4.21m	13.83ft/4.21m	13.83ft/4.21m
Empty weight	13,402lb/6,079kg	13,405lb/6,081kg	14,914lb/6,765kg	16,309lb/7,398kg
Gross weight	19,100lb/8,664kg	19,100lb/8,664kg	n/a	n/a
Max speed	468mph/753kph	483mph/776kph	465mph/748kph	460mph/740kph
Ceiling	40,000ft/12,192m	41,600ft/12,680m	40,000ft/12,192m	38,500ft/11,735m
Range	1,390mls/2,237km	1,390mls/2,237km	2,504mls/4,030km	2,200mls/3,541km

Republic P/F-84 Thunderjet; First Flight: 28 February 1946
As familiarity with the jet engine and its potential application began to take hold in the United States during the latter stages of the Second World War, a General Operational Requirement (GOR) was issued on 11 September 1944 for a mid-wing fighter with a maximum speed of 600mph (965km/hr) and a combat radius of 850 miles (1,367km). It was to carry eight .50-in calibre machine guns or six .60-in calibre guns, but these figures would be adjusted down to six and four guns, respectively when weight became an issue.

When the requirement and the technical capabilities of the day were compared the performance figures were also reduced, to a combat radius of 705 miles (1,134km) when the capabilities of the stipulated engine, the axial-flow GE TG-180 gas turbine engine were taken into account. This engine was under development by the Air Technical Services Command and in production it would be manufactured by the Allison Division of General Motors as the J35. The AAF was determined to stimulate a rapid growth in US jet propulsion units and match this engine with a suitable airframe.

The studies were contemporaneous with the Lockheed P/F-80 and the North American Aviation P/F-86 and on 11 November 1944, the AAF issued a letter contract to Republic Aviation for its proposal without a competitive bid. That was unusual but the AAF considered both the GOR and Republic's proposed design to be superior to the Lockheed P/F-80 and as the company had great success with the P-47 Thunderbolt it pressed ahead.

The initial letter contract dated 4 January 1945 supported 100 aircraft including 25 test and 75 production airframes but the total for test and production would be adjusted to 15 and 85 respectively for a design which bore the service designation P-84, or F-84 after the 1948 designation change. Republic moved quickly to secure a full contract and hosted a mock-up inspection at its Farmingdale, New York, plant which was conducted over 5-11 February, from which the AAF Materiel Division requested only a few minor changes.

Initially, Republic had planned to put a jet engine in its P-47 airframe but it quickly became apparent that a completely new design was necessary. The design incorporated a cantilever, low, straight

Ordered on the basis of Republic's success with the P-47 Thunderbolt, the F-84 Thunderjet proved to be a robust and resilient fighter, interceptor and ground attack aircraft. Here, F-84E-1-RE Thunderjets of the 2750th ABW Flight Test Division are seen before going to the 27th FEW. (USAF)

and laminar-flow wing with cantilevered, horizontal tail surfaces mounted halfway up the vertical fin. The airframe was to be of all-metal, duralumin skin with a nose air inlet for the turbojet engine, the first time that had been seen on an American jet. Enclosed by a teardrop canopy, the pressurised cockpit included an ejection seat. An airbrake was installed in the lower fuselage.

The first definitive contract awarded on 12 March included three XP-84 aircraft and a static test model as well as spares and various test items but development evaluation at the NACA's Langley Field Laboratory showed some serious problems. The stabiliser skin buckled under test and longitudinal stability fluctuations in the high-speed tunnel became evident on semispan models. An overriding concern was the excessive growth in weight and by July 1945 a revised design was necessary with gross weight set at 13,400lb (6,078kg) and these changes were incorporated on the third prototype, redesignated XP-84A.

A further problem involved delayed engine tests, a not unfamiliar challenge as US manufacturers wrestled with production of reliable and effective engines, keeping the first two prototypes waiting at Muroc Dry Lake. By early 1946, however, the first prototype was ready for flight, powered by a J35-GE-7 turbojet with a thrust of 3,750lb (16.68kN) and taken into the air on 28 February by Major William A Lien. Named Thunderjet, an appropriate successor to the P-47 Thunderbolt, it was the first newly-minted US fighter flown since the end of the Second World War and proved a worthy addition. The second prototype flew in August and on 7 September 1946 it set a new US air speed record of 611mph (983km/hr). But that was exceeded later that day by a British Gloster Meteor with a speed of 615.78mph (990.8km/hr). However, Republic could bask in the news that on 15 January it had received verification of the order for 15 YP-84As and 85 production P-84Bs.

The desire to show performance and seize the world speed record prevented comprehensive test and evaluation of the second XP-84 and slow engine deliveries hampered the desired flight test programme. The third prototype, the XP-84A, made slow progress, evaluating several modifications which would go into the production aircraft. Mindful of costly development changes that had to be integrated with the P-80 Shooting Star after it entered production, the Air Force advised Republic that unless the bugs could be ironed out on the pre-production aircraft it could result in cancellation. Nobody wanted then what would later be known as concurrency, with development still underway as production began – a potentially time-consuming and costly process. The blank-cheque mentality of the recent war years seemed a distant memory.

The determination to modernise the Air Force toward an all-jet complement of combat types encouraged a major effort to track and solve emerging problems but the low production rates for engines and the general shortage of parts slowed development. That affected preparation of maintenance personnel through lack of equipment for training and familiarisation, activities planned for Muroc. As tests slowly progressed, deliveries of the YP-84A with the Allison engine, wingtip tanks and six .50-in machine guns, four in the upper forward fuselage and two in the wings, began in February 1947 and were completed two months later.

With a specification virtually identical to the YP-84A, differing only in having eight retractable rocket launchers beneath each wing from the 86th aircraft onward, all 226 P-84Bs had been delivered by June 1948. The first aircraft went to the 37th, 48th and 49th Squadrons of the 14th FG at Dow AFB, Maine, from 7 November 1947, with the last to this unit arriving in February 1948. The 14th had gone to Muroc to continue testing but despite three aircraft being lost it appeared that the type operated better under the colder conditions.

Operational difficulties persisted and the aircraft encountered structural failure with the type grounded on 24 May 1948 until inspections revealed the need for a redesigned fairing and from June the designation changed from P-84B to F-84B. A special modification programme began in May 1949 which included modification of the aircraft's wings and more than a hundred structural and engineering changes. These were applied to the 191 F-84C aircraft delivered between April and November 1948, equipped with the J35-A-13 engine instead of the A-15, together with special refinements designed into the electrical systems, looms and circuitry.

The F-84C went first to 20th FG at Shaw AFB, South Carolina but operational difficulties increased and both variants experienced heavy losses as accident rates soared to a post-war high. Structural and material failures were frequent but pilot error was a significant cause for many crashes. This pushed the Air Force to re-evaluate pilot

A flight of F-84B-21-RE Thunderjets, the nearest one (46-548) served with the 49th FS, 14th FG at Dow AFB, Maine in late 1947. The F-84B was the first production variant, equipped with machine guns supplemented with underwing rocket packs. (USAF)

training for this and all fighter jets and industry was recruited to help produce booklets and briefing charts to enhance familiarisation. Factory representatives would visit the units to explain the significant differences between piston-engine and jet-powered fighters, adding new elements to the basic Air Force training curriculum.

In 1948, production switched to the F-84D of which, with the more powerful J35-A-17D engine producing a thrust of 5,000lb (22.24kN), 154 were delivered between November 1948 and April 1949. Production issues still haunted the Thunderjet and even before delivery of the first F-84D Republic participated in a complete programme review. It became clear from unit reports, interviews and examination of maintenance and operating records that none of the B and C variants had delivered to expectation. It became clear that the only solution was to perform a complete retrofit to redress shortcomings in manufacturing and installation. Overall production was a year behind the contractually obligated schedule and tough decisions had to be made.

A radical solution would be to cancel the programme but as procurement of the F-84D had already taken place, the costs of cancellation would be more than continuing to accept the remainder of that production run, half of which had already been delivered by the time that consideration was aired. As a solution, between 2 February and 6 March 1949, the Air Force conducted special tests to determine whether incremental improvements with the newly-minted D models would correct many of the shortcomings observed from data on the B and C variants. Moreover, there was also analysis of whether the F-80 or the F-84 best suited service as a fighter-bomber, the role for which the Thunderjet had been built.

The results from these tests held at Wright-Patterson AFB, Ohio, and Eglin AFB, Florida, were reassuring, verifying that the D model had absorbed enough of the improvements to warrant continued production and that the 'F-84 range, acceleration, versatility, load-carrying ability, high-altitude climb, and level flight speed exceeded that of the F-80'. However, it also reported that the F-80 was superior in shortness of take-off roll, low-altitude climb and manoeuvrability and that, while ground crews found advantages with improvements in their procedures, the additional time taken to service the front-end accessories on the engine compromised efficiency. Overall, judgement came down in favour of continuing the programme but not beyond the variant then in production, the F-84E. That decision would also be rescinded in light of further development which would come within the chronological period of Volume 4.

New Variants
First flown on 18 May 1949 and accepted on 26 May, the F-84E was the first breakaway variant from the standard aircraft as reflected through the first three production variants. It was a response to Air Force demands for longer range and improved performance and improved maintainability at a unit and general overhaul level. The fuselage was increased in length from 37.42ft (11.40m) to 38.58ft (11.76m), affording more room in the cockpit, with empty weight increasing from 9,860lb (4,472kg) on the F-84D to 10,205lb (4,629kg) on the F-84E. Improved wingtip tanks were fitted as well as 230USGal optional tanks on two underwing bomb shackles inboard of the landing gear. It also had a sophisticated A-1B radar gunsight, later replaced with the A-1C, and improved weapons capacity and operability. The contract for the F-84E was issued on 29 December 1948 and after general endorsement of the Thunderjet programme, additional funds were provided for pre-production improvements.

The first 100 aircraft were the first of any type assigned to the Mutual Defense Assistance Programme (MDAP). That was created on 6 October 1949 just six months after the formation of NATO, prompted by tension over the blockade of Berlin and the ensuing airlift. The MDAP was the first US military foreign and legislative act of the post-war era and provided security for the Western Alliance through the provision of weapons and military aircraft to NATO partners. It is sometimes compared with the Lend-Lease programme of the Second World War but it was different in that it did not require any money to be paid back. On 26 August 1954 the MDAP would be rebadged as the Military Assistance Programme (MAP) and by 1967 the United States had supplied £3.7 billion worth of weapons and services to shore up the defence of Western interests.

By July 1951, all 843 F-84Es had been delivered. However, the dispersal of F-84 Thunderjets to foreign bases under the MDAP initiative exposed the type to different standards of maintenance in other countries and to various environmental conditions. Together with B, C and D variants, more than half the Thunderjet operational inventory was out of commission in April 1950, starved of spares and ancillary equipment largely due to stringent defence budget cuts and poor engine life. It had been believed that the J35-A-17 engine would operate for 25 hours per month and for 100 hours between overhauls but the global distribution and difficulties in supporting high rates of serviceability and maintenance levels made those targets impossible to achieve.

Largely due to priorities in building up non-US, NATO forces, Air Force funds were required to expand GE's Allison production line using additional engines to compensate for lower-than-expected targets. Expanded resources for the Korean War from 1950 brought no respite and MDAP commitments stalled attempts to increase dispersal and operational support for Southeast Asia. But the type would earn credit for being 'the best ground-support jet in the theatre' by pilots and maintenance crew alike. Which could be said to have been judgement on the parlous state of the rest. In addition to the US Air Force, 13 NATO and non-NATO countries procured the F-84 Thunderjet and some operated them into the 1960s.

The final variant of the Thunderjet appeared in 1951 but as it was the last of the straight-wing F-84 types, it will be included here. It evolved from a requirement to support long-range ferry operations for overseas deployment. That had been evaluated on 22 September 1950 when two modified F-84Es, rebadged as EF-84Es, made a nonstop flight across the North Atlantic from England to the United States. Piloted by Colonel David C Schilling, one aircraft performed three inflight refuellings over Scotland, Iceland and Labrador using the British probe-and-drogue system over a total flight duration of 10 hours and two minutes. Lieutenant Colonel William Ritchie piloted the second aircraft but failed to connect with the tanker over Goose Bay and took to his parachute when the aircraft ran out of fuel.

The onset of the Korean War and hostile moves from Russia and China pressed a need for developing the capability of moving large numbers of aircraft across the Atlantic at short notice. Deployments to overseas bases in Europe and the Middle East were seen as conditional on the prevailing tensions, the view taken that it was better to keep units at home stations for rapid deployment as required. NATO was in its early days and would only gradually move toward a more permanent system of rotation through foreign locations, bases owned by the host country with a political decision to allow their use by American units.

In the same week that Schilling made his westabout crossing of the Atlantic, 89 F-84Es flew from Bergstrom AFB, Austin, Texas, to Fürstenfeldbruck, south-west of Munich. They were there to replace the P-47s and made the transfer across four days without complications. This and other exercises in long-range flight were used

Preserved at the National Museum of the US Air Force this F-84G-16-RE is painted in the colours of Colonel Joseph Davies of the 58th FBW when it served in Korea. (NMUSAF)

by the Air Force and the engine manufacturer to evaluate incremental improvements in performance and reliability. In a series of eight flights to evaluate both the aircraft and the functionality of the Allison J35 engine, a single F-84E logged a total flight time of 23 hours and five minutes in a 24-hour period.

This was part of an accelerated service evaluation where 15 aircraft completed 50-hour tests within a single week and at Turner AFB, Georgia, five aircraft flew 105.45 hours in a single day at an average of 21 hours of flight for the J35 engine. Tests with the J33 for the F-80 and the J35 in the F-84 progressed through deployment of both types and by the end of 1949 the two engines had exceeded 600,000 hours in the air with time between overhauls up to 500 hours. Production had been accelerated as improvements were incorporated and by 1950 Allison had delivered a total of almost 10,000 engines since the end of the Second World War.

By this date the Thunderjet was clearly suited to the role of ground attack and, with better and more powerful

A formation of Thunderjets, the nearest two of which are from the P-84B-16-RE block lot with the third from the P-84B-11-RE lot. (USAF)

engines, was also to carry tactical nuclear weapons. For this, and for inflight refuelling with the US flying-boom system with a receptacle in the port wing, Republic developed the F-84G, considered as an interim variant before the development of the swept-wing F-84F Thunderstreak. With a 5,600lb (24.9kN) thrust Allison J35-A-29 engine and provision for 4,000lb (1,814kg) of external stores (down 500lb (227kg) on the E variant), the F-84G was the first US single-seater capable of carrying nuclear weapons, which required considerable adaptation with loading equipment.

The G also had a multi-framed canopy replacing the unframed canopy of earlier variants, a change retrofitted to several earlier Thunderjets, which can cause confusion on identifying variants from images alone. To afford some relief from hands-on flying, it had an autopilot and a new A-4 gunsight from the 86th article, instrument landing system from the 301st and new weapons support equipment. The fuselage of the G variant was six inches (15.2cm) shorter than the F-84E and the overall height was three inches (7.6cm) less than all preceding Thunderjets. Maximum take-off weight had grown from 22,463lb (10,189kg) for the E to 23,525lb (10,67kg) and the top speed was up slightly at 622mph (1,001km/hr).

Deliveries began in July 1951 and the nuclear capability was added incrementally after rollout but there were delays in getting the type operational due to engine problems in early production lots. The 31st Fighter-Escort Wing at Turner AFB, Georgia, was the first unit to receive the F-84G but the flying-boom inflight refuelling equipment did not enter the SAC inventory until 1952. The majority of F-84Gs were supplied to MDAP countries with only 789 of the 3,025 eventually delivered going to the US Air Force, the last of this variant being rolled out in July 1953. From this date the Air Force began to introduce the Low Altitude Bombing System (LABS), a technique for safe delivery of nuclear weapons whereby the aircraft approaching the target would pitch up, release its bomb, continue a half loop, roll to a heads-up attitude at the top and depart the target in the opposite direction at maximum speed to escape the ensuing blast.

The F-84 production line with an Allison J35 engine on its transport dolly. (Republic Aviation)

In July 1953, the 81st Fighter-Interceptor Wing converted to nuclear capability and took its F-84Gs to RAF Bentwaters in Suffolk, England, as the first overseas deployment of this aircraft for NATO in a tactical nuclear role. A few weeks later, on 29 August 1953, 17 F-84Gs flew from Albany, Georgia, across the Atlantic to RAF Lakenheath, Suffolk, a flight of 4,485miles (7,216km) nonstop, refuelled by KC-97 tankers along the way, making this the longest mass movement of fighter-bombers and the greatest distance flown by single-engine jet fighters. These inflight refuelled operations became the backbone of future Air Force overseas deployments, significantly reducing response time to unanticipated threats in foreign countries.

The record of the Thunderjet in the Korean War is dealt with in Volume 4 but the type found application in a variety of tests for new technology. On 2 June 1954, F-84Gs took part in Project ZELMAL (Zero Length and

A mix of F-84 Thunderjets, some with aft fuselage tail sections removed and displaying trailing edge control surfaces including the flaps. (USAF)

Mat Landing), undertaken by the Martin Company to evaluate the use of rocket-assisted take-off (RATO with arrested landing on a pneumatic landing mat). Part of an exploratory effort to find ways of getting aircraft airborne without the aid of a runway, it was never deployed operationally but several aircraft types received RATO-assisted take-off for laden aircraft, including B-47 bombers and some transport types.

Although projected as an interim variant, more F-84Gs were produced than any other of the straight-wing Thunderjets, accounting for more than two-thirds of the 4,439 delivered. The Thunderjet would provide the base design from which new and significantly greater potential would be realised through the swept-wing F-84F Thunderstreak and the RF-84F Thunderflash photo-reconnaissance variants, both of which will be dealt with in Volume 4. As will the further story of the straight-wing Thunderjet in the Korean War, a type that had done so much to provide the US Air Force with its first jet fighter-bomber and to expose unique difficulties facing conversion from propeller-driven combat aircraft.

Table 4: Republic P/F-84 Thunderjet Specifications

	P/F-84B	F-84C	F-84E	F-84G
Span	36.41ft/11.09m	36.41ft/11.09m	36.41ft/11.09m	36.41ft/11.09m
Length	37.41ft/11.40m	37.41ft/11.40m	38.58ft/11.76m	38.08ft/11.60m
Height	12.83ft/3.91m	12.83ft/3.91m	12.83ft/3.91m	12.58ft/3.83m
Empty weight	9,538lb/4,326kg	9,663lb/4,383kg	10,205lb/4,629kg	11,095lb/5,033kg
Gross weight	16,475lb/7,473kg	16,584lb/7,523kg	n/a	18,645lb/8,457kg
Max speed	587mph/945kph	587mph/945kph	613mph/987kph	622mph/1,001kph
Ceiling	40,750ft/12,421m	40,600ft/12,375m	43,220ft/13,173m	40,500ft/12,344m
Range	1,282mls/2,063km	1,274mls/2,050km	1,485mls/2,390km	n/a

North American Aviation F-86 Sabre; First Flight: 1 October 1947

Arguably the most famous US fighter of the immediate post-war period, the swept-wing F-86 is an icon in aviation history. It began as an Air Force version of the Navy's XFJ-1 Fury, a straight-wing contender for production to fill a requirement contested by the McDonnell FH-1 Phantom and the Vought F6U-1 Pirate. Designated NAA-134 by North American, it was a low-wing monoplane with laminar-flow wings and a General Electric J35-GE-2 engine with a nose inlet. The Navy was aware of Germany's experimental designs with swept wings but wanted to minimise risk and adopt a conservative approach. The Air Force had a different view and sought to exploit the results from analysis of German experimental projects.

Three XP-86 prototypes were ordered by the Air Force on 18 May 1944, before the full extent of German swept-wing research became known. Overall, the XP-86 was similar to the straight-wing Navy proposal and at first had that wing. When North American engineers L P Greene, Ray Rice and Ed Schmued got their hands on the German data, they convinced their boss, Lee Atwood, that such a wing would give the XP-86 a 70mph (112km/hr) speed advantage over the XFJ-1 Navy contender. The Air Force prioritised speed over anything else but the straight-wing design was the one presented at a mock-up on 20 June 1945. The Air Force required further persuasion to adopt a swept wing. Some advice it was getting in design of the experimental Bell X-1 transonic research aircraft warned of instability and there appeared to be few

The epitome of future fighter designs, the first USAF swept-wing combat aircraft was the North American F-86A, developed from an initial design for the straight-wing Fury for the US Navy. (Adrian Pingstone)

solutions the Germans could find to counter this effect, especially on the Me 262.

The General Operational Requirement issued the previous month stipulated a top speed of 600mph (965km/hr) and in seeking to achieve that the thinner wing on the XP-86 had a thickness ratio of 10 percent. This would extend the critical Mach number to 0.9 compared to 0.8 on the P-80 Shooting Star and 0.76 on the P-51 Mustang. What the Air Force wanted was a combat fighter and the engineering data which produced the mock-up predicted a top speed of only 582mph (936km/hr) at 10,000ft (3,048m). Wind tunnel tests in early June showed that the airframe design, although of high fineness ratio, could not produce the performance required, or the predicted speed that even the F-84 was promising.

Greene, et al, pored over the German documents and translated them into English, gaining insight to the methodology in those designs relevant to reducing the drag rise through the swept leading-edge and slightly compromising performance to regain some stability. The NAA designers did have some home-grown experience with swept wings from the Curtiss-Wright XP-55, an unsuccessful wartime research project with a canard layout, rear-mounted engine and two vertical tails. Three were built as research aircraft but two crashed and it was abandoned.

In compensating for loss of stability at low speed, Greene concluded that an automatic leading-edge slat on each wing was the most likely solution, one that the Germans had decided upon but never successfully developed. Greene proposed this idea to NAA's Vice-President and chief engineer Raymond Rice in August 1945, receiving approval later that month to conduct wind tunnel tests for which a 23 percent scale model was prepared and placed in the tunnel on 18 September. With the rudimentary addition of a strip of stretched metal around the wing's leading-edge, low-speed runs showed a distinct advantage while removal of the strip revealed a considerable performance increase in the swept wing for high-speed runs, raising its critical Mach number.

From this work a report was issued titled RD-1369 and submitted to the Air Force on 1 November showing considerable improvement with the swept wing but adding that this would probably delay the project by up to a year. To verify their conclusions, the model was refitted with a Me 262 wing shape and the planform inherited for the XP-86. No other aircraft had proved altogether successful with this type of wing but there was a solution, the addition of an auto-operated slat which was both radical and seminal. However, the performance was dependent on selecting the appropriate aspect ratio, one of 1:6 providing better range while 1:5 improved stability. In a further series of tunnel tests conducted between 26 October and 13 November, the longer wing proved to be satisfactory and that was incorporated into the proposal, which was accepted on 1 November 1945.

But that was not the end of the story. Further tests in parallel with detailed airframe design left the exact configuration undecided pending additional tests and calculations from the results. A considerable amount of work was required to balance disadvantages with advantages and much of the development work on swept wings conducted by North American would cascade through the industry over the next few years. And it required a lot of people to solve the contradictions in design and test. Peak employment on the NA-140 project was reached in January 1946 with the equivalent of 445 full-time engineers on the payroll.

In March, the wing design was finalised, with an aspect ratio of 4.79:1, a 35-degree leading-edge sweep and a thickness/chord ratio of 11 percent at the root and 10 percent at the tip. With the fully automatic slots operated by the aerodynamic forces on the wing, when open at slow speeds the airflow increased over the upper surface, increasing lift. When they were closed at higher speeds it minimised drag for optimum performance. Initially, they opened at 150mph (241km/hr) and closed at 333mph (536km/hr) but this compromised manoeuvrability and from the 160th F-86A, the speed band for opening and closing the slots was changed to 132–207mph (212–333km/hr).

A definitive contract for three prototypes (45-59597 to 45-59599) was awarded to NAA on 20 June 1946, followed by a production contract for 33 aircraft on 20 December. The full set of engineering drawings had already been passed over to the body shop and work could begin on building the first XP-86A prototype. The specification anticipated an empty weight of 9,243lb (4,192kg), a gross weight of 13,311lb (6,038kg) and a maximum all-up weight of 16,438lb (7,456kg). Top speed was now projected to be 635mph (1,022km/hr) at 16,000ft (4,877m), a service ceiling of 44,200ft (13,472m) and a climb to 35,000ft (10,668m) in 12 minutes. Engineers cautioned that these figures would be compromised by an increase in weight, however.

During the autumn of 1946 further and more extensive tests were carried out by the NACA in the 16ft (4.8m) wind tunnel at the Ames Aeronautical Laboratory, Moffett Field, endorsing the optimistic predictions of the design team. There were other modifications which would gradually appear on the production line but it was clear the Air Force had a winner-in-waiting. The high-speed tests ended in February 1947 and attention switched to the new Cooperative Wind Tunnel at the California Institute of Technology's facility in Pasadena. By May, NAA reported that it had completed 1,500 hours of low-speed tunnel tests of its own with three months of that added from Ames, making this one of the most comprehensive tunnel-test programmes in US aviation history to this date.

The F-86 would prove to be a generation ahead of existing jet fighters and the design innovations introduced by NAA were used elsewhere. In its report on the engineering applied to the F-86, the company noted that:

A double-skin structure with hat sections between layers extends from the centre section to the outboard edges of the outer panel fuel tanks, replacing the conventional rib and stringer construction in that region. Tapered skins have been used to save weight. The inboard upper skin, for example, is 0.25in (0.63cm) thick at the wing root and 0.64in (1.62cm) at the joint where it meets the outboard skin; the latter tapers…to 0.32in (0.81cm) at the wing tip. Specially-equipped milling machines, using carbide-tipped fly-cutters up to 12in (30.48cm) in diameter were set up in North American's main plant to solve the new fabrication problems presented by these skins. The most complicated skin, on which three operations are required to obtain compound tapers, is completely machined in only 45 minutes.

Use of 75S aluminium alloy throughout to provide a maximum strength-weight ratio has also complicated the production process, as have the extremely close tolerances required by both structural and aerodynamic considerations. As an example, a tolerance of only 0.002in (0.005cm) is allowable on external rivet heads; this makes it necessary to shave about 15 percent of them after assembly. The need for maximum fuel space in the new thin structure has further complicated design. This requirement, heightened by the rapid increase in fuel consumption accompanying higher

F-86A-5-NA Sabre fighters in final fit-checks at North American Aviation. (NAA)

logged 15,332 man-hours between 22 November 1943 and 3 June 1945 on the design study alone. Completion of the project absorbed 801,386 engineering hours, 340,594 drafting hours together with 2,738 primary and 3,816 changed drawings plus 6,488 requested engineering orders.

Power struggles

The first prototype XP-86A rolled out on 8 August 1947 with a J35-C-3 engine built by Chevrolet and producing 3,750lb (16.68kN) of thrust but it would be re-equipped with the more powerful J47-GE-3 engine. The aircraft displayed was almost identical to the production aircraft except that it had no armament. Following inspection a week later it was taken by truck from the Mines Field factory alongside International Airport, Inglewood, California, to Muroc Dry Lake where it arrived on 10 September for reassembly and pre-flight checkout.

The man selected to take the aircraft into the air was George Welch, a distinguished AAF pilot who had heroically raced to his P-40 Warhawk at Oahu when the Japanese bombed Pearl Harbor on 7 December 1941. He attacked three Aichi Val dive-bombers, shooting one down together with a Mitsubishi Zero which crashed on Wahiawa, becoming the first AAF pilot to shoot down a Japanese combat aircraft. In his service career Welch shot down a total of 16 Japanese aircraft and received the Distinguished Service Cross. In 1944 he became a test pilot for North American Aviation. Welch had already flown the prototype XFJ-1 Fury on 27 November 1946 when flight tests with the XP-86 began.

Phase I testing began on 1 October 1947 but a flight planned to last 10 minutes lasted four times as long when Welch attempted to deploy the landing gear and the nose leg had refused to lower, resisting all attempts to get it down and locked. Running low on fuel and coming in nose high, as Welch put the main wheels down the shock deployed the nose gear and the landing occurred as planned. Category I tests were the manufacturer's verification of flight compliance with the general specification and that was completed in 30 hours before Category II began when Major Kenneth Chilstrom took it over for 11 flights, completed in 10 hours 17 minutes of flying time between 2 and 8 December.

As installed for the tests, the J35-A-5 engine had a thrust of 3,920lb (17.57kN). In general, flight reports were positive, with noise and vibration levels markedly lower than other jet aircraft and good control characteristics but with a need to hold the nose up 13 degrees on take-off to prevent the aircraft sinking back. The aircraft would become airborne at 125mph (201km/hr) after a ground run of 3,020ft (920m). But weight was a problem, empty weight having grown to 9,730lb (4,413kg) and gross weight increased to 13,395lb (6,076kg). None of the flight test results indicated a need to alter the overall dimensions of the production type, the P-86A.

The Air Force was pleased when it demonstrated a top speed of 618mph (994km/hr) at 14,000ft (4,267m) and a service ceiling

speeds, has been the factor chiefly responsible for the growth in size of fighter aircraft that has marked the post-War period. The XF-86, for example is some 40 percent heavier than the F-51H.

The special sandwich wing construction was developed by Richard Schleicher, the company's chief structural designer. The traditional method of structurally testing the whole wing by way of extrapolated measurements from small sections was impossible due to elastic instability. The selected method was to test a scaled-down wing with proportionately reduced metal gauges and this helped achieve for the aircraft a history largely without structural failure. In several ways, and in this example in particular, the F-86 represented a new approach to the use of materials, stress-mapping and in testing for potential failures. All of which enhanced reliability and reduced losses.

Because of the structural design of the fuselage and the resonant frequencies caused by altered airflow maps on the external wing surfaces, the original idea of wing-mounted speed-brakes was not suitable and substituted by a large, folding door brake but eventually that was abandoned in favour of two hinged doors, one each side of the fuselage. The design allowed the pilot to use them to temporarily reduce relative speed-to-target rates for better gun aiming, or to help recovery from a dive, even to decelerate in a high-g turn.

In other considerations and for ease of maintenance, the aft section of the fuselage behind the wing trailing edge root could be detached after removing four bolts, leaving the aircraft standing on its tricycle landing gear affording full access to the engine and its tail pipe. It would take ground crews less than an hour to change engines. All of this was managed during development by the lead project engineer A F 'Tony' Weissenberger together with his assistant Art C Patch who, along with their teams during an intense period of activity, of 41,300ft (12,588m), exhibiting good stall characteristics and a noticeable warning 6.9mph (11.1km/hr) before the onset. Good recovery was noted and the final report from Major Chilstrom asserted that it was clearly the best jet fighter that had yet been offered to the Air Force. On that basis, Category III testing began in January 1948 which consisted of high Mach number tests, measurement of stick forces per g level at forward and aft centre of gravity locations, position error calibration, longitudinal stability tests, roll rate calibration and control inputs being assessed through different configurations.

In February a further and more comprehensive series of Category III tests provided more detailed and specific numbers for a very wide range of parameters and with various elevators and different centre of gravity positions. On one of those flights there was another nose wheel incident but the aircraft recovered. The following month the aircraft was delivered back to the plant where minor rework was carried out and a few subtle changes made. Meanwhile, a second production order had been placed on 28 December 1947, adding 190 to the previous order for 33, all of these being F-86As.

The first flight through Mach 1 was achieved on 26 April 1948 when Welch took it into a shallow dive, the first US combat aircraft to achieve that. The aircraft had only a moderate tendency to pitch up at Mach 1 but production aircraft were limited to Mach 0.95, or 668mph (1,075km/hr), below 25,000ft (7,620m) for safety but with no limits above that altitude. Fifty years after that event, a book was published that claimed Welch conducted the first Mach 1 flight two weeks before Yeager took the Bell X-1 through the sound barrier in level flight on 14 October 1947. Welch never said he had done that, the claim by the author being based on eyewitnesses and little more than rumour. There is abundant technical analysis to show that the underpowered XP-86 was incapable of reaching Mach 1 but the myth persists.

The first production type was designated F-86A-1, NAA-51 (47-605) and made its first flight on 20 May 1948, the month before a contract was awarded for a further 333 of this variant. It was the first type to use the 5,200lb (23.13kN) thrust J47-GE-1 turbojet engine and the Air Force took delivery of this and the second aircraft (47-606) on 28 May. These two aircraft remained at Inglewood to assist with production development activity but 47-605 did not go to an Air Force station until 29 April 1950 when it was assigned to Wright-Patterson AFB before retirement to Griffin Air Depot in May 1952 after logging 501 flying hours.

Remarkably, although empty weight had grown to 10,077lb (4,571kg), the more powerful engine increased its top speed to 673mph (1,083km/hr) and the enhanced performance encouraged the Air Force to make a public display its new jet fighter. Previous record-breakers in 1946 and 1947 had been specially prepared aircraft but this time the Air Force wanted to use the new standard production fighter to show off its potential. The selected event was the National Air Races at Cleveland, Ohio, where the FAI had established strict controls for an official world speed attempt, which included a 1.86 mile (3km) course over which two runs had to be made during one continuous flight below 165ft (50m) to allow the photographic cameras to accurately time the event.

On 5 September 1948 a crowd of 80,000 gathered to watch the attempt as Major Robert L Johnson of Air Materiel Command piloted F-86A-1 47-607 through six passes over the course. Three of the runs were discounted because the timing equipment failed, on a fourth run a Navy FJ-1 Fury tripped the cameras and on two attempts turbulence compromised maximum speed. With an

On display at the National Museum of the US Air Force, this F-86A is marked up in the colours of 49-1236 flown by Lieutenant Colonel Bruce Hinton who became the first F-86 pilot to shoot down a MiG-15. (NMUSAF)

An F-86A-5-NA (49-1225) with underwing drop tanks while serving with the 4th FIG. (USAF)

average of 669.48mph (1,077km/hr) on the two timed runs there was insufficient gain to establish a new record. But the public had experienced a spectacular show at the fastest display ever mounted.

Major Johnson got another chance when he returned to Muroc for another set of runs in quieter air. On 15 September he flew 47-611 to a new world record of 670.981mph (1,079.6km/hr). Equally telling and of greater significance was the report from North American that every aircraft coming off the production line exceeded that speed in pre-delivery tests! Performance would only get better as more refined and powerful J47-GE-7 and -13 engines were integrated on the production line. The definitive speed for production F-86A-1 aircraft was set on 23 September 1948 when 47-610 achieved 677mph (1,089.3km/hr) at sea level with a maximum Mach number of 0.885. A service ceiling of 47,000ft (14,325m) was registered and a stall speed of 119mph (191km/hr) established.

The airframe production line at North American had been cleared when the Navy reduced its order for the Fury from 100 to 30, the last of that type being delivered in April 1948 but sluggish engine production slowed delivery of the F-86A-1s. By the end of 1949 the problem had been solved and deliveries were up to schedule, now involving 3,000 workers employed on manufacture, assembly and testing. The aircraft block ordered in May 1948 were designated F-86A-5 and carried the company project number NA-161, the first of which (48-129) was delivered in March 1949.

Previous aircraft had the characteristically curved windscreen with flush-fitting gun muzzles which had doors that would open in 0.05 sec when the trigger was squeezed to fire the guns and close again after each burst, maintaining the smooth exterior surface of the airframe. The F-86A-5 had a new, V-shaped windscreen and the doors were removed to ease maintenance, the exit tubes now fitted with plastic covers being shot away on first use but in service the covers were usually removed. It also had a jettisonable canopy, a heating system for the gun compartment, a stainless steel oil tank and improved, flame resistant lines.

Having established basic characteristics of the type, in early 1949 Air Materiel Command received 10 F-86A-1s for additional pre-service tests before the aircraft could be fully integrated with operational units. The first two, 47-606 and 47-607, were kept at North American where they would participate in production development; 47-608 went to Eglin AFB, Florida, for cold tests in the climatic hangar; 47-609 went to the NACA's Ames facility at Moffett Field where its cockpit was equipped with connections to 144 data points for heavily instrumented tests; 47-610 went to Edwards AFB for stability checks; 47-611 was dedicated to armament tests; 47-616 was the pacing aircraft for flying alongside other test aircraft; 47-619 was retained at North American for structural integration tests; and 47-621 and 47-622 were assigned to engine control tests.

Engines were a critical item in the late 1940s and despite production problems both Allison and Pratt & Whitney were busy competing for full involvement with contenders in the turboprop and turbojet fields, despite a late start. But engine development shared production problems with traditional reciprocating engines, Pratt & Whitney's greatest achievement to date being the Wasp Major which powered the Boeing B-50 in stunning, long-distance flights, including a non-stop circumnavigation of the globe in 94 hours and one minute on 2 March 1949 (see Volume 2).

For the F-86 however, there was consideration to replacing the General Electric J47 with the Allison J35-A-17 used in the F-84E and this was installed in the first XP-86 prototype, increasing gross weight to 13,250lb (6,010kg). In tests conducted between 28 November and March 1951 performance remained about the same as that achieved with the F-86A-1 but with a slightly better range. There was insufficient advantage to justify the cost in switching engines.

Sabre into service

The first USAF unit to receive the F-86A-1 was the 94th Fighter Squadron (the 94th Fighter-Interceptor Squadron from 16 April 1950) of the 1st Fighter Group at March Field, California, between February and March 1949. This unit bore the famous 'Hat in the Ring' insignia from the First World War and was quickly followed by the 27th and 71st Squadrons, with 83 aircraft fully operational by the end of May. During February, at March AFB the Group held a contest to name the F-86 and a group of officers selected 'Sabre', which was official on 4 March 1949. The next Fighter Groups to get the Sabre were the 4th based at Andrews AFB, Maryland and the 91st at Albuquerque, New Mexico. There was both purpose and poignancy in these assignments.

By the late 1940s the three cardinal points of potential vulnerability for the defence of the United States were the survival of the political leadership in Washington, DC, the massive aviation production facilities in the Los Angeles area and the design and development of nuclear weapons at Los Alamos. The initial unit deployments

This F-86E-10-NA (51-2832) served with the 25th FIS, 51st FIG at Suwon AB, Korea. (USAF)

covered defence for all of those locations, places made all the more vulnerable after Russia detonated its first atomic bomb and opened the possibility of catastrophic damage from Russian Tu-4 bombers on one-way suicide missions to key targets.

Armament fitted to the F-86A-1 consisted of six .50-in (1.27cm) M3 guns operating at 1,100 rounds per minute with 267 rounds per gun. The pilot had a Mk 18 gunsight with lead computing capability set to the wingspan of the target aircraft, the pilot positioning the attitude of the aircraft so that the target appeared within a circle of six diamonds on the reflector glass. When the diameter of the circle was the same as the target and held in frame for one second, the required lead was computed and the guns could be fired. After the first 530 F-86A-1 aircraft were delivered, the last 23 were equipped with the A-1CM as well as to the F-86A-5 variant.

The A-1CM worked with an AN/APG-30 radar with a sweep range of 450–9,000ft (137–2,743m), installed within the top of the nose inlet. Below about 6,000ft (1,829m) its automatic lock-and-track capability became erratic due to ground clutter, at which point a manual ranging and sight dial could be used by the pilot. In operation, the target image was projected on to an armoured glass and when that was acquired a light indicated the time to track continuously for one second before firing. The A-1CM could be used for guns, rockets or dropping bombs. When retrofitted with the A-1CM and the AN/APG-5C radar, initial production F-86A-5s became FG-86A-6 and when receiving the A-1CM and the AN/APG-30 they were designated F-86A-7.

Although designed as a dog-fighting interceptor, the Sabre could carry bombs in place of jettisonable fuel tanks, either two 100lb (45kg), 500lb (227kg), or 1,000lb (450kg) bombs. It could also carry 750lb (340kg) napalm tanks, 500lb (227kg) cluster munitions or chemical dispensers. They could also carry as an alternative, eight detachable, zero-rail rocket launchers each equipped with 16 x 5-in (12.7cm) rockets fired singly or in clusters from the outboard position first and working inward. But this was no ground-attack aircraft. The compromised performance when carrying external ordnance was considerable, two 1,000lb (450kg) bombs in lieu of jettisonable fuel tanks reducing the combat radius from 330 miles (531km) to 50 miles (80km). For this reason, unit commanders were reluctant to employ the type on any task other than its prime, design mission.

The F-86A packed an internal fuel load of 435USgal in four self-sealing tanks, of which 196USgal was in the forward fuselage wrapped around the air intake duct, a 105USgal aft tank in the rear fuselage and two 67USgal tanks in the wing roots. Additionally, two 120USgal drop tanks could be carried under the wings and ferry flights undertaken with 206.5USgal tanks. The aircraft was designed to be as compact as possible, reducing airframe weight, limiting the external dimensions to reduce drag and enhancing the engine power/mass ratio. The fuel system was integrated fully in this design process, which was a unique aspect of aeronautical engineering compared to earlier projects.

Special consideration was given to the efficiency of the operating systems, to pilot comfort and safety and to his protection. An aluminium alloy steel plate weighing 51lb (23.5kg) was set behind the seat with another panel in front of the instrument panel and an armoured glass windscreen protecting the pilot from frontal attack. Air conditioning and pressurisation used hot air bleed from the engine compressors with the temperature selectable between 40 degrees F (4.4 degrees C) and 80 degrees F (26.6 degrees C). A T-14E-1 ejection seat was installed and incorporated a height adjustment for the pilot by means of a lever located on the right of the headrest, requiring the pilot to lift off the seat for it to go up or to add weight for lowering. The ejection process was rudimentary and compromised by the tight fit of the canopy and the low front frame, and it was useless below 1,000ft (300m).

To activate, an emergency O2 bottle was turned on, the pilot would lower his head and pull up the right handgrip to jettison the canopy which would slide back along the rails. Now sitting upright, the pilot would lock the harness with the left handgrip, bringing his feet back to the footrests and bracing his arms on the armrests. He would then push his head back against the headrest with his chin tucked in. In that position the pilot would squeeze the ejection trigger located under the handgrip, igniting the catapult which would fire the seat together with its occupant up and back away from the aircraft. This sequence would automatically disconnect the pilot's umbilical and connectors and, once clear, he would release the safety harness, kick away the seat and manually activate the parachute after descending to a safe height.

Voice and two-way communications were provided by the AN/ARC-3 VHF command radio set with a line-of-sight range of about 30 miles (48km) at 1,000ft (300m) and 135 miles (217km). The AN/ARN-6 radio compass which could accept voice and code signal commands provided position finding and homing to a range of up to 200 miles (322km). There was also an AN/APX-6 IFF identification

A delightful shot of two F-86A-5-NA of the Arizona ANG, the nearest of which has its air brakes deployed. (USAF)

set which operated a challenge-and-response tone when 'painted' by friendly radar. In the event of a crash, this device would automatically engage a self-destruct signal to prevent the device falling into enemy hands.

Several line-improvements to production aircraft provided a better canopy with improved defrosting from the 100th aircraft in May 1949 to prevent ice from accumulating above 37,000ft (11,277m). A liner coating was applied to the nose intake duct fairing to halt rain erosion and earlier airframes were retrofitted with this. From the 160th aircraft off the line, a different wing slat mechanism was introduced eliminating the lock for a fully automatic operation. A complete rewiring of the cockpit on F-86A-5s from 49-1007 onward simplified both production time and servicing effort on the ground. A different trailing edge design was introduced on the 282nd aircraft with a shorter-chord aileron and higher elevator boost and these collective changes were made in parallel with the new J47-GE-13 engine.

In all, the Air Force received 554 F-86A aircraft but there were other variants including the F-86B, a proposed redesign with deeper fuselage for additional fuel and larger tyres, 188 being ordered before it was cancelled in favour of an equivalent number of the A variant. The F-86C was the concept developed as the YF-93A with a completely redesigned fuselage and flush side-intakes (see Appendix). It was never developed out of the prototype stage. The F-86E emerged in production prior to the F-86D, an all-weather interceptor, which was a completely different Sabre and the first of the second-generation Sabres which will be covered in later volumes.

The last major variant of the fighter-bomber types, the F-86E was a development of the initial production model incorporating a new tailplane with elevators connected for linked and coordinated

Table 5: North American Aviation F-86 Sabre Specifications

	XP-86	P/F-86A	F-86E
Span	37ft/11.27m	37.08ft/11.30m	37ft/11.27m
Length	37.5ft/11.43m	37.5ft/11.43m	37ft/11.27m
Height	14.75ft/4.49m	14.75ft/4.49m	14ft/4.26m
Empty weight	9,730lb/4,414kg	10,093lb/4,578kg	10,555lb/4,788kg
Gross weight	13,790lb/6,255kg	15,876lb/7,201kg	16,346lb/7,414kg
Max speed	599mph/964kph	679mph/1,093kph	679mph/1,093kph
Ceiling	41,300ft/12,588m	48,000ft/14,630m	47,200ft/14,387m
Range	750mls/1,207km	660mls/1,062km	848mls/1,365km

movement. The first flight of the initial F-86E production model (50-579) took place on 23 September 1950 with the same J47-GE-13 engine fitted to the later F-86As. The Air Force accepted the first two in February 1951 where they were assigned to the 33rd Fighter-Interceptor Wing. This and subsequent variants of the fighter-bomber variants designated F-86F and F-86H, together with the F-86D, F-86K and F-86L interceptors will be covered in Volume 4.

Northrop F-89 Scorpion; First Flight: 16 August 1948

The origin of this all-weather fighter emerged toward the end of the Second World War with detailed requirements including a combat radius of 600 miles (965km) and a top speed of 530mph (853km/hr) at sea level. It was required to carry the .50 or .60 calibre M3 machine gun with a flexible mounting for up to 15 degrees of movement, automatic gun-laying being preferable and with a minimum of four forward and two rearward facing guns and interchangeability for 20mm cannon. Sufficient ammunition was required for 20 seconds

The YF-89A Scorpion (46-679) made its first flight on 25 September 1950 after a lengthy gestation from the original XP-89 which had taken to the air on 16 August 1948. (USAF)

of fire per forward-firing gun and 10 seconds for the rear-facing guns. The aircraft was to carry a minimum of two bombs each up to 1,000lb (453kg) and provision for a minimum of eight rockets.

The requirement for the all-weather fighter had been set out on 23 March 1945, as described in the introduction to this chapter, but that was changed later that year from a propeller-driven engine to a twin-jet configuration. It got the attention of Bell, Consolidated (Convair), Douglas, Goodyear, Northrop and Curtiss-Wright and they had each submitted designs by March 1946. The AAF wanted a fighter capable of operation in the harshest of weather, defending the skies of the northern zones, the Arctic Circle and specifically the Territory of Alaska, which would become a State in 1959, from attack cross the North Polar regions.

Consolidated submitted a concept which incorporated a delta-wing design and which would re-emerge later as the F-102 while the Douglas entry was an adaptation of its XF3D-1 Skyknight, a carrier-based, all-weather Navy fighter. Curtiss-Wright put up a large, four-jet aircraft which the AAF liked, ordering two prototypes under the designation XP-87 (see Appendix), the company's parlous financial position and empty order book of this most iconic of all US aircraft manufacturers getting the attention of the selection board.

Northrop received a letter on 28 August 1945 inviting it to submit designs for penetration, interceptor and all-weather fighter requirements, the three classes defined through evaluation of needs in the post-war air force. Northrop submitted the tailless, flying wing XP-79B of 1942 which had been subcontracted to a small company that failed its client. Taken back in-house, it had been completed in 1945. It had the pilot in a prone position and was powered by a single Westinghouse engine for a calculated top speed of 630mph (1,014km/hr) at 45,000ft (13,172m) but any chance of its potential use crashed with it on 12 September 1945. A radical, flying wing concept, it was this that Northrop had initially proposed to the AAF.

On 29 November 1945, Northrop presented two separate configurations for the all-weather proposal, one a tailless concept derived from earlier work which had resulted in the XP-79B and another with a more conventional layout. Northrop offered four separate designs designated A, B, C and D and these were evaluated by the AAF's Aircraft Projects Section. The company had two tailless, flying-wing designs (C and D) and two conventional configurations (A and B). The post-evaluation reports rated the two conventional designs best, with preference going to A on the basis that it proposed two TG-180 engines rather than the Westinghouse 24-C of configuration B.

In the ratings assessment, Northrop came top with its design, scoring 71.8 compared with 71.4 for Goodyear, 70.7 for Curtiss-Wright, 70.3 for Douglas, 56.0 for Bell and 37.3 for Consolidated. Notable were the highly commendable scores of 70.0, 73.2 and 73.4 for Northrop designs, B, C and D respectively. Curtiss-Wright had already received a contract for the XP-87 but Northrop was selected for the XP-89 calling for two prototypes (46-678 and 46-679), the in-house designation being N-24. Northrop was advised of the decision on 18 March 1946 but a week later the ratings scale was changed, raising the Northrop A submission to 72.6 and the Goodyear number to 71.7. Curtiss-Wright and Douglas suffered under the new scale, their new scores dropping.

The final contract proposal was adjusted on 25 March 1946 and formalised on 10 April with the official date of the contract agreement being 3 May. Designed around the J35-GE-3 engine it was modified to accept the Allison J35-A-9 and would be built at Hawthorne, California. The Aircraft Laboratory at Wright Field would conduct tests on a straight wing configuration compared with two swept at 30 degrees and 45 degrees respectively to determine general performance and potential top speeds. There was negligible advantage with a 30 degree wing sweep but some marginal improvement with the 45 degree wing, the decision being made to adopt the straight wing while holding the swept wing in reserve for later consideration.

The straight wing was recommended on the basis of functionality including aerodynamic efficiency and the requirements of armament, wing loading and the need for external stores. Total lift and stall characteristics were found to be better with the straight wing while the swept wing was less effective for the carry-through structure. In addition, a thin, nine percent aerofoil was judged to be an acceptable alternative to the general trend for wings of 12–15 percent thickness ratio. Moreover, heavy armament and store loads were impossible with a swept wing, compromising both balance and centre of gravity, while shifting the loads inboard on such a wing would result in enhanced interference drag in the air flow around the fuselage.

The selection of a thin wing created problems with structural design and layout, compromising the design of the main landing gear and accommodation for wing bending loads. Selection of a particularly large main gear wheel with a diameter of 46 inches (116.8cm) and a high-pressure tyre brought challenges with stowage within the thin wing, which had a multi-spar construction with heavily formed skins without supplementary stiffening for bending and torsion loads and with fewer ribs to shape the skin allowing larger fuel tanks. The conventional monocoque fuselage had bolt-on nose and tail sections, assembly building outwards from a centre wing torque box with a vertical split along the centreline for reduced manufacturing time by providing better access for installation of the plumbing, wiring and systems equipment in each half.

The Northrop F-89 Scorpion was the result of a requirement for an all-weather, two-seat fighter and would enter service in the early 1950s as the first of its kind with the US Air Force. (USAF)

As development of the design proceeded, the AAF became concerned by reports of the Tu-4 strategic bomber, a reworked Soviet production-line version of the Boeing B-29, examples of which had been made available when they landed in Russia as part of Allied war operations. Dated 8 October 1946, a change in requirements due to these considerations required that the forward-firing guns be flexibly mounted for a minimum 15 degrees of motion away from the longitudinal axis and that 20mm cannon should be installed with sufficient ammunition for 20 seconds of fire. This eliminated the tail turret which had previously been a component of the Northrop design and refocused the mission on the ground-attack role with a requirement for steep dive angles.

This highlighted diverging opinion on just what constituted an all-weather fighter. One school advocated the traditional role inherited from Second World War practices, limiting the fighter to operate at night and in bad weather; the other school saw it as a multi-role, all-weather combat aircraft equipped for roles as diverse as day/night defence against enemy attack, ground-support and dive bombing. The diversity of opinion caused a considerable rework of the basic design with further changes imposed to include moving the radar operator from a rear position closer to the pilot, a revised canopy to include both crewmembers and substitution of aluminium for magnesium in the wings. There were also serious objections to the way the fuel was contained in wrap-around tanks directly above the engines.

At the mock-up inspection on 25 September, the unfavourable situation regarding multiple changes threatened the very survival of the programme. At a key meeting on 13 November 1946, Jack Northrop himself met with AMC personnel to discuss the ramifications of the changes, presenting an alternative and safer fuel system arrangement but noting the potential ramifications on costs and labour assignments. Here too, opposing viewpoints were made when the AAF Fighter Branch expressed concern both at the state of development and of the changes requested, asserting that it was unwise to press forward with a production order before critical matters had been addressed.

At a further mock-up inspection on 17 December 1946, the latest configuration was examined with all the requested changes and not a few compromised choices. The original fuel system arrangement was retained but separated from each engine by self-sealing firewalls which consisted of a corrugated fibreglass panel with a 0.5-inch (1.27cm) sheet of 24ST aluminium and a stainless steel cooling jacket. But the engine staff inspecting the mock-up were still not satisfied that this was a safe configuration, as no other US combat aircraft had this arrangement where the fuel was carried alongside the engine exposing the design to fire risk.

Additional change requests were made as the AAF became bogged down in new requirements which delayed progress on the XP-89 and disrupted a proper flow of engineering and design work. On 10 April 1947 a summary of change requests included a reversal from magnesium to thick aluminium sheet, a proposed power operated control system and raised vertical stabilisers on the fin. Very quickly, the aircraft became embroiled in the struggle to get a 70-group Air Force and in an environment of tight fiscal constraints it was tagged as a potential failure. As late as 7 June 1948 with design changes sill in a state of flux, a mock-up inspection would find 262 changes for the XP-89 (at this date on the cusp of becoming the XF-89) with 60 required for the production aircraft.

The AMC was firm in its resolve to have a gun-laying turret on the aircraft and Northrop designed into the layout a fuselage break to accommodate such a 'barrel', but that was not to be. Then, on 28 July 1948 a request was made to fit the second prototype, redesignated YP-F-89A with an afterburning J35-A-21 engine with a thrust of 6,800lb (30.2kN) instead of the 4,000lb (17.8kN) thrust J35-A-9/15 engine installed in the XF-79. The XF-89 was moved to Muroc AFB on 26 July 1948 with initial taxi trials conducted by Northrop test pilot Fred C Bretcher Jr on 12 August, with a high-speed run culminating in a fleeting lift-off before the first true flight four days later. On that day the aircraft had a weight of 31,900lb (14,470kg), the aircraft becoming airborne at 125mph (201km/hr) with a 20-degree flap deflection. Leaking hydraulic fluid and fuel cut short an otherwise successful flight and Belcher landed with flaps stowed 11 minutes later.

The blended intakes for the F-89 provided some boundary layer bleed in a configuration of fuselage and duct similar to that of the Bell P-59 Airacomet. (NMUSAF)

Re-evaluation

As Phase I testing was being conducted the Air Force decided to have a fly-off competition between the Curtiss-Wright XF-87 Blackhawk, the Northrop XF-89 and the Douglas XF3D-1 and that was conducted at a 'conference' on 6–8 October 1948. The Douglas design got top marks for maintainability followed by the Curtiss-Wright design and then Northrop but on speed the XF-89 was fastest followed by the XF-87 and then the XF3D-1. Stability trials put those in reverse order but since the XF-89's instability was considered correctable with a different power control system, it mattered little. Against these three, and largely for comparison only, the XF-90 was brought under review but since it was at this date only a paper concept it could not rate credible scores.

Also under evaluation, for yet another complete revision of what defined an all-weather fighter, were comparative studies with the P-61, F-82, F-84, F-86A, F-80C and a modified F-80 which would be designated F-94. The AMC and the top brass in the Air Force were looking to define an all-weather fighter for the period 1952–1954 and this would eventually result in the F-102 and then the F-106. Under the pressing requirement for an interim all-weather solution, the general trend was to go with the XF-89 concept as the least deficient of all the contenders! But there were some seminal configuration changes still to be defined for the production aircraft.

Completed in January 1949, the first 32 test flights were flown satisfactorily but with standard ailerons and those revealed an instability which had been put down previously to the need for an improved power control system and improved feedback 'feel' for the pilot. In fact, it required a new form of control surface which was introduced for the next flight by fitting 'decelerons' in place of the standard ailerons. These were split horizontally so that they could be used as ailerons, flaps or speed-brakes, occupying the outboard 42 percent of the wing trailing edge, leaving the inboard 58 percent with double-slotted flaps and effectively providing full-span flaps for landing and take-off. They would remain standard for all production aircraft, a prescient forerunner to the split speed-brakes fitted to the Northrop Grumman B-2A and the B-21.

The Phase I testing was completed on 14 June 1949, the date Phase II tests started, two weeks after a request for studies of a photographic reconnaissance variant, identified at Northrop as the N-54 model with the service designation RF-89A. It would never be adopted but the tests with XF-89 were disrupted when it crash-landed on Muroc Dry Lake during its 64th flight on 27 June 1949, necessitating a new landing gear. To get it back a crane lifted the aircraft from the surface while engineers attached a new set and had it as towed away to the hangar, resuming flight tests on 15 October 1949.

During February 1950, the prototype was moved to the Hawthorne plant where, devoid of any markings, it was used as a secret enemy aircraft in the film *Jet Pilot* starring John Wayne and Janet Leigh. Tragedy struck on 22 February when it crashed during a high-speed run as part of a test demonstration before Air Force inspectors waiting at Northrop Field. Test pilot Charles Tucker was killed but Arthur Turton in the rear seat parachuted to safety after the wing broke off before the crash. Tail flutter had led to its failure which caused loss of longitudinal control and production was suspended pending further investigation of the type's structural integrity.

But the XF-89 had been severely deficient in power and the second prototype, the YF-89A (Northrop model N-49) was powered by the 6,800lb (30.2kN) thrust J35-A-21A engines. Fuselage length increased by 3ft (0.91m) to 53.43ft (16.28), wingspan was slightly reduced to 56.16ft (17.11m) due to slimmer tip tanks and six 20mm cannon were in the nose. It achieved its first flight on 27 June 1950 but production of the operational F-89A was already under way, with three delivered by the end of the year when production was suspended pending verification of technical changes from Northrop.

This view of the F-89 displays the wide-track main landing gear and the short nose gear leg giving the aircraft a squat appearance. (NMUSAF)

The F-89 could carry two AIR-27A Gene air-to-air rockets with nuclear warheads and four AIM-4C Falcon missiles. (NMUSAF)

The first of 48 F-89As (49-2431) had taken to the air on 25 September 1950 but many changes were in the offing and the programme was burdened by the dual demand of the Air Force for it to support a tactical ground-attack role as well as its prime function as an all-weather, two-seat fighter. The six 20mm cannons would use the AN/APG-33 radar and the A1-CM gunsight as a functional part of the Hughes E-1 fire-control system. For ground attack, 16 x 5in (12.7cm) HVAR-type rockets would be carried with up to 3,200lb (1,451kg) in bombs on fixed stores points, as opposed to retractable installations featured on the prototypes.

Several changes were introduced as a result of flight tests with the F-89A and a new fairing was added to smooth airflow above the engine exhausts as well as a switch from 75STAL to 24STAL for the horizontal tail skins. There was a considerable amount of attention paid to the need for weight reduction. The F-89 was a big aircraft and there were many changes including to the tip tanks necessary to resolve issues of unstable airflow in that area. Overall, the F-89A was in essence an interim pre-production design and only 18 were completed and 11 accepted by the Air Force, the remaining 37 being reassigned to the F-89B production lot.

The F-89B was virtually identical to the F-89A, with the jet wake fairings, the Hughes nose gun and with the addition of all-weather instrumentation and cockpit lighting, an instrument landing system (ILS), a Sperry zero reader, which allowed the pilot to fly a predetermined altitude or heading, and Lear F-5 autopilot, developed in cooperation with Northrop and this being the first aircraft to use it. The F-5 was more than a convenience. With operational sorties of up to four hours in duration, some relief for the pilot was a clear advantage in keeping him alert. Production of all 37 F-89Bs was completed in September 1951 but since most were upgraded F-89As, there were a great many line-changes and engines variants fitted to different aircraft as delivered.

The first of 164 F-89Cs flew on 18 September 1951 with the more powerful, 5,600lb/7,400lb (24.9kN/32.9kN) thrust Allison J35A-33 engines with reheat but these continued to cause trouble and led to difficulties integrating with operational units. Not all the engine problems were design or engineering issues as servicing and maintenance had its own issues too. One frustrating effect of the low intake location was a tendency to suck material from the ground to mash compressor blades and cause flameouts or worse, earning the type its label as the world's biggest vacuum cleaner while some applied the nickname 'Garbage Gobbler'! Inlet screens were provided but at high altitude these accumulated ice which clogged them and brought its own hazards.

The first F-89Bs had gone to Air Defense Command's 83rd and 84th Fighter-Interceptor Squadrons with the 78th Fighter-Interceptor Group at Hamilton AFB, California, beginning February 1951. The F-89C entered service with the ADC's 74th Fighter-Interceptor Squadron at Presque Isle AFB, Maine, in January 1952 but it was an uneventful induction. On 25 February 1952, an F-89C disintegrated in the air and this was followed by a spate of further accidents where structural failure was clearly the cause. The reason was largely due to the stress load factors applied to different categories of aircraft type.

An interceptor would usually be stressed to a 5.67g level while day fighters designed for high manoeuvrability and dog-fights would be designed to a limit of 7.33g. As a high-altitude, all-weather fighter the F-89 would stall before encountering the 5.67g load factor but the pilots flew them as fighters where higher g-loads were normal and the powered flight controls gave little notice that they were over-loading the airframe. Without feedback from the stick force, pilots were unable to get a feel for angular acceleration, only for the rate of the manoeuvre and would frequently use excessive elevator for a given requirement.

The F-89 was subject to many change requests in the extended period between its inception and operational deployment, not least because of uncertainty as to precisely what the requirement for a two-seat, all-weather fighter should be. (NMUSAF)

While the pilot-induced stresses were a reason for the accident, the cause was within the structural design and manufacture of the wings. Considerable time and attention were paid to unravelling the complexities of loads, stresses and fail-rates for different parts of structural assembly. Test data on wing bending moments and on torsional stiffness showed that in the aircraft's wing the reduction in these factors induced higher twist values which increased the air loads on the outer portions and that increased root bending some 30 percent higher than the previous limit load analysis revealed. The key to solving the problem was in changes to a combination of material and production techniques used by Northrop. The solution would be to redesign the wing attachment fittings, machined and formed from fabricated plate with a control on the grain direction and the addition of a spar to improve bending and torsional strength at the higher loads, plus the addition of fins on the tip tanks to reduce torsional loads.

For these and other reasons, the aircraft had been taken into service too quickly. Rushed from production to delivery before there were sufficient crewmembers proficient in the skills required for flying and operating these complex aircraft, accident rates were high. The advanced role the aircraft was designed to fill included equipment new to most veterans of all-weather flying and

The F-89 was powered by two Allison J35 turbojet engines as shown here at the National Museum of the US Air Force. (NMUSAF)

the combination of this new aircraft, the first of its kind for the Air Force, together with the advanced electronic equipment needed for its mission, produced a difficult combination to manage. The E-1 system was new and incorporated technology still in its infancy, pressed into operational use before the bugs could be ironed out.

The changes effected by the reviews and investigations following the sequence of accidents in 1952 provided lessons that would be applied throughout the US combat aircraft programme and after the wing modifications had been implemented, the aircraft became the safest aircraft in the inventory with fewer major accidents than any other type. The operational story of the Scorpion, a name applied due to its similarity in profile to the poisonous arachnid of that name, really begins with the F-89D and a few subsequent variants. That story will be picked up on Volume 4.

Table 6: Northrop F-89 Scorpion Specifications

	YF-89	F-89A	F-89B	F-89C
Span	52ft/15.84m	56ft/17.06m	56ft/17.06m	56ft/17.06m
Length	50.45ft/15.36m	53.45ft/16.28m	53.45ft/16.28m	53.45ft/16.28m
Height	17.66ft/5.38m	17.5ft/5.33m	17.5ft/5.33m	17.5ft/5.33m
Empty weight	25,846lb/11,732kg	23,645lb/10,725kg	24,064lb/10,915kg	24,512lb/11,118kg
Gross weight	43,910lb/19,918kg	36,560lb/16,583kg	36,782lb/16,684kg	37,619lb/17,063kg
Max speed	603mph/970kph	642mph/1,033kph	642mph/1,033kph	642mph/1,033kph
Ceiling	35,500ft/10,820m	51,400ft/15,666m	50,000ft/15,240m	51,400ft/15,666m
Range	1,759mls/2,816km	875mls/1,400km	690mls/1,100km	875mls/1,400km

Lockheed F-94 Starfire; First Flight: 16 April 1949
Although numerically following the F-89 Scorpion, the Starfire was an evolution of the TF-80C trainer (T-33A from 5 May 1949) which was itself a development from the P/F-80 Shooting Star. The search for an all-weather, radar-equipped fighter called for a two-seat aircraft, one crewmember being the radar operator and the existing stretch of the F-80 made it a logical choice, albeit one with only an interim and somewhat limited potential.

Lockheed's Kelly Johnson and Russ Daniell came up with the concept early in 1948 and raised the possibility of adapting the existing P-80 airframe. On 8 October 1948 the Air Force issued a General Operational Requirement which defined the need for an early production all-weather interceptor and six days later, after formal approval to develop the F-89 Scorpion, Lockheed was directed to come up with a faster solution and adapt the TF-80C for a production aircraft that could enter service by the end of 1949. As the Scorpion was a completely new design and much more capable than the F-94, that aircraft would not be available for operational deployment until the early 1950s.

For the Lockheed variant, the nose had to be lengthened to accommodate the radar and four .50-in guns and the rear fuselage had to be widened to allow the 4,000lb/6,000lb (17.79kN/26.68kN) afterburning Allison J33-A-33 engine to be installed. The tail was made taller and some fuel capacity was lost due to the need for space to accommodate the additional equipment but this made it necessary to carry underwing or centreline tip tanks on each wing to supplement the fuel load. A formal mock-up review was held on 24 February 1949 and the initial Model 780 was shipped to Van Nuys airport where it would begin flight trials, rather than the busy Burbank airport. Lockheed named the new aircraft Starfire.

Designated XTF-80C (48-356) the first was flown on 16 April 1949 with Tony LeVier at the controls and the rear seat occupied by Glenn Fulkerson. There were no surprises and the aircraft was quickly accepted, the basic airframe having already been flown in a variety of adaptations as both single and dual-seat versions of the Shooting Star. The second XP-80A had been conducting experimental engine tests and the J34 was installed but proved difficult to operate. The initial aircraft had been identified as ETF-22A (the 'E' standing for

First of its type and an evolution from the F-80 and the T-33, the first of two YF-94s (48-356) emerged as a two-seat, all-weather fighter equipped with APG-32 nose radar and tip-tanks for range. (USAF)

'Exempt' and not 'Experimental') and redesignated YF-94 before hosting a wide range of different and conflicting designations.

The first production F-94A made its initial flight on 1 July as the first all-weather fighter to enter operational service with the US Air Force. During the February mock-up review, Johnson had proposed an F-94B which would have a nose section accommodating rockets. There was a tide of opinion moving through senior staff levels that rockets were the firepower of the future and that guns were unsuited to very fast interceptions and dog-fight encounters. Johnson wanted his Starfire to be ahead of the rest and believed that rockets were better for night and all-weather missions. That concept was put on hold and the 'B' suffix was applied to the next evolution of the A model with the YF-94B, the reworked 19th production F-94A, which made its first flight on 29 September 1950. But tests showed that neither variant could be truly regarded as all-weather fighters.

Meanwhile, the more advanced proposal from Johnson had received little enthusiasm due to the development of the larger and more capable F-89 Scorpion but that programme was having its own problems. The Air Force slowly tipped toward the more capable Lockheed concept and the Model L-188 testbed was bought under the designation YF-97. This would be redesignated F-94C so as not to encourage belief in the fiscally-constrained civilian leadership that it was embarking on a completely new project, which in effect it was since the capabilities of that variant were far beyond those of the F-94B.

The YF-97/F-94C made its first flight on 18 January 1950 and the Air Force immediately ordered 617 aircraft into production. As a privately funded development, the concept would prove a winner. Powered by a 6,250lb/8,300lb (27.8kN/36.9kN) thrust J48-P-5

One of the 357 F-94Bs (50-955), a variant which made its first flight on 28 September 1950. (USAF)

or P-5A afterburning engine, it had thinner wings with increased dihedral, a sweptback horizontal stabiliser, aft dive flaps, a drag parachute and a longer nose with a radome in a retractable shield. Replacing gun options, the nose would carry 48 x 2.75-in (6.98cm) folding-fin aerial rockets (FFARs), half of which would be carried within a ring of tubes around the nose and 12 in each of two cylindrical pods carried under the wings.

The F-94C would have more fuel, de-icing kit on the horizontal stabiliser, single-point refuelling for speed, the Hughes E-5 fire-control system and a Westinghouse W-3A autopilot. The E-5 consisted of the AN/APG-40 radar and the AN/APG-84 computer. In the fully militarised production F-94C was officially designated as such on 12 September 1950. But once again the 150-hour qualification tests for the Pratt & Whitney engine delayed certification, eventually passed in May 1952. There were also some development issues with airframe systems and improvements to the breech mechanism were required for the rockets to achieve significantly better accuracy.

The F-94C would not be accepted before May 1952 and by the following month 10 test aircraft had produced results which at first were disappointing, with speeds considerably lower than the F-89. Late tweaks and changes produced better flight characteristics and control functions but reliability still plagued the programme. The P-5 engine continued to have flameouts when firing trials required full rocket bursts above 25,000ft (7,620m). With 12 rockets fired simultaneously, near-flameouts occurred and the aircraft's speed slowed appreciably. Improvements came slowly and it would be some time before the wing pods were installed carrying the Aeromite-developed FFARs, each with 9.5ft (2.89m) tubes projecting 6ft (1.82m) beyond the wing leading-edge.

As the F-89 Scorpion achieved operational status, by late 1952 the Air Force considered cancelling the Starfire and cut the total production order for the F-94C from 617 to 387. A key decision not to cancel the whole programme was the need to keep Lockheed in production during the Korean War. Induction to operational service began with the 437th FIS at Otis AFB, Massachusetts, but not before March 1953 and that will be covered in Volume 4, along with its operations during the Korean War.

An early F-94A (49-2498) with a clear lineage back to the P-80 displaying the single-piece canopy for the two crew seats and the only slightly modified air intakes for the J33-A-33 afterburning engine. (NMUSAF)

Table 7: Lockheed F-94 Starfire Specifications

	F-94A	F-94B	F-94C
Span	38.92ft/11.86m	38.92ft/11.86m	42.41ft/11.37m
Length	40.08ft/12.21m	40.08ft/12.21m	44.5ft/13.56m
Height	12.66ft/3.86m	12.66ft/3.86m	14.91ft/4.54m
Empty weight	9,557lb/4,335kg	10,064lb/4,565kg	12,708lb/5,764kg
Gross weight	12,919lb/5,860kg	13,474lb/6,112kg	18,300lb/8,301kg
Max speed	606mph/975kph	606mph/975kph	640mph/1,029kph
Ceiling	49,500ft/15,088m	48,000ft/14,630m	51,400ft/15,666m
Range	1,079mls/1,736km	905mls/1,456km	1,275mls/2,051km

5
ROLES AND RESPONSIBILITIES

While post-war defence strategy would focus on the long-range strategic bomber, the fighter was considered the prime defence asset in bringing down approaching intruders in any future conflict. Correctly assessed at the end of the Second World War, the probability of a direct air attack on the continental United States was highly unlikely for the foreseeable future. The Soviet Union did not have the capacity or the equipment to mount such an offensive and assessments of when they might have that capability were optimistically placed in the mid-1950s at the earliest. Nevertheless, mindful of the shock when Japan struck Pearl Harbor on 7 December 1941, plans were set down for how to provide warning of any similar surprise and to respond accordingly.

Air Defense Command had been established on 21 March 1946 commanded by Lieutenant General George E Stratemeyer charged with setting up a national alert system of radar sites for early warning and aircraft to defend the continental United States. At the time that consisted of four understrength fighter squadrons and a role which in reality consisted of operating a single training unit equipped with Second World War radar sets. The general belief among politicians and the general public was that the strategic bombing capability so ably demonstrated between 1943 and 1945 would prevent any adversary attacking the United States. The Air Force thought so too but nuanced it differently and also sought to provide an effective continental defence system – just in case.

When the Air Force became independent, late in 1947 the Supremacy plan was activated, providing an aircraft control and warning (AC&W) screen protecting the entire continent of North America. The plan was to set up 411 radar stations, 374 in the United States, at a projected cost of $400 million. In March 1948 at a conference in Key West, Florida, the Joint Chiefs gave the Air Force responsibility to set that up. There was as little an appetite for this among politicians as there was for a strong air force, many believing that an entrenched belief in the Soviet Union being an aggressive predator was a scaremongering tactic to extract more money.

But in February 1948 Stalin ordered communist elements in Czechoslovakia to conduct a *coup d'état* and set up a pro-Moscow regime for fear that they would lose an upcoming democratic election. General Lucius D Clay, the US military governor of West Germany warned that a Third World War could break out any moment and with 'dramatic suddenness', General Spaatz ordered air defences be set up for the north-east and the north-west of the United States and in Alaska, which was at the time a Territory and not yet a State of the Union. At this date, only one radar station was in operation in the continental USA, with four in Alaska operating only a few hours each day. In response, one fighter group was sent to Alaska and one to McChord AFB, Washington.

Within a month some existing radar sites in the northwest had been reactivated and some old equipment renovated in the northeast. Realising that the atomic development centre at Albuquerque, New Mexico needed defending, the Air Force began to set up similar Supremacy systems there. Ironically, Congress passed over the opportunity to vote on funds for the new system when it was presented in June 1948 and again in 1949. Realising that funds would never be approved for the $400 million required, the Air Force decided to shelve Supremacy in favour of a less ambitious scheme involving a radar-based alert system.

Known as Modified, this was a proposal for what was termed a Permanent System of 75 radar stations and 10 control centres in the US and Alaska. The 85 installations were to be ready for full operations by 1952 and cost $86 million but the rationale for their operation was as an information source rather than an integrated air defence network tied to assigned air bases and fighter squadrons. No new equipment would be procured, the entire network being dependent on old but usable radar sets. Congress approved this and the Air Force set about expanding the temporary network, work on this having been underway since the previous year in the optimistic hope that they would receive funds. In a cynical overview of the entire debacle, the interim programme was officially known as Lashup, as it sought to provide some degree of protection to the important California, Northwest and Northeast areas.

Air defence was a priority in the post-war Air Force, epitomised by this P-61B-10-NO (42-39556) from the 2nd FS. (USAF)

TECHNOLOGY@WAR VOLUME 2

A Lockheed P-80A (44-86064) assigned to the 1st FG with the aft fuselage section removed. (USAF)

Lashup used funds from other Air Force programmes to find the money and used land areas then occupied by other government departments on which to put the radar equipment. While rating the overall probability of a Russian attack highly unlikely, there was little or no intelligence regarding the true state of Russia's strategic warfighting capabilities. This had already resulted in the first major effort to get information using aircraft to conduct penetration flights with radar and other equipment, a capability explored in Volume 2. But the most alarming indication of a future threat came on 29 August 1949 when Russia detonated its first nuclear device at Semipalatinsk.

The urgency this provoked came on the heels of the Soviet inspired, communist takeover of Czechoslovakia in 1948 and the Berlin blockade of 1948–1949. With funds available in 1950, when by June America had plunged into a war with North Korea, a significantly accelerated pace saw completion of the 44 Lashup stations by the end of that year. Tests had shown both positive and negative results of Lashup. In spring 1948, SAC bombers simulated a bombing run on the Seattle, Washington, area to evaluate the acquisition and response times of early warning radar and to measure the effectiveness of the relevant fighter wings. A year later, under Operation Blackjack a test was conducted of the Northeastern Lashup defences and many were found to be inadequate. In November 1949, Operation Drummerboy probed the Northwestern area and found much the same.

To bring forward the Permanent System, fighter units were integrated and dispersed to stations and bases aligned with the early warning net in a seminal shift in procurement and fighter/fighter-bomber requirements as well as deployment. All of which is explored in Volume 4 but suffice to say here that it focused minds on exactly what mission the post-war fighter requirement should be designed for. This would result in a rapid evolution of gun and rocket air-to-air weapons with which to equip the new jets and bring about a revolution in the way air-to-air combat was practised.

Command and Leadership

A direct influence on the evolution of US air power strategy, on the philosophy dictating national and international defence policy and on the structure of commands down to unit level were three seminal events in this period: the opening shots in the escalating tension of Cold War adversarial stand-offs and confrontations between East and West; the development of a bipolar nuclear-armed world dominated by threats of war; and by the formation of NATO, with the United States as its *de-facto* leader exercising political and to some extent financial control with technologically advanced weaponry.

A Republic F-84B (45-59577) of the 37th FS at Dow AFB, Maine in 1948. (USAF)

Within that structure, the US Air Force matured from operating subsonic, propeller-driven combat aircraft to jet aircraft which would soon dash to their targets at supersonic speed and engage in combat at speeds greatly in excess of anything seen during the Second World War. Moreover, the migration from machine guns and cannons to guided and unguided rockets and missiles was well underway and the development of combat tactics came as a result. But it would not fully mature until the experiences of jet-on-jet combat became possible during the Korean War (1950–1953).

The Cold War grew out of ideological differences between communist and capitalist countries, including those making the transition from colonialism to independence in a process that had largely begun by fighting Germany and Imperial Japan during the Second World War. It is not appropriate to engage here with an extended description of the several steps taken to divide the post-war world into polarised and hostile sectors but the stand-off and the tensions produced by these events would shape the requirements for combat aircraft on both sides of the divide and serve to gather like-minded democracies into a united front to communist belligerence.

One determined effort successfully administered by the United States provided a unifying coalition for European defence with the North Atlantic Treaty of 4 April 1949. According to Lord Ismay, its first Secretary General, its primary goal was to 'keep the Russians out, the Americans in and the Germans down'. As a robust form of Atlanticism, the concept of uniting the common interests of the people of North America and those of Europe, it worked on several fronts and it is relevant here because that played a significant role in changing the requirements for combat aircraft on both sides of the Atlantic Ocean and north of the Tropic of Cancer, which is 23.4 degrees north of the equator.

The formation of NATO came about as a result of previous agreements which began when the Treaty of Dunkirk, a defensive pact, was signed by the UK and France on 4 March 1947, to which were added the three Benelux countries of Belgium, the Netherlands and Luxembourg in 1948. To these five countries were added as NATO signatories the United States, Canada, Italy, Portugal, Norway, Denmark and Iceland. More countries would join later. The basic tenet of the defence pact unified the signatories to come to the aid of any member attacked by a non-member state with full military force. The combined interest in cooperative security extended to a growing commonality of equipment and some standardisation in munitions and conventions for identification.

A universal standardisation of military terminology and procedures was agreed and air forces across the member states began to adopt US practices. There was an expectation among NATO countries that they could tap into longer US production runs and acquire aircraft at less cost than they could produce them domestically, albeit forfeiting potential foreign sales relinquished to the United States. In the 1950s, standardisation in calibre of aircraft armament would begin and that would be equally applied to military and naval forces. There was also a mandatory agreement on aircraft marshalling signals, a common recognition code for any NATO aircraft landing at any NATO-member airfield. Made all the more relevant because of the multi-lingual membership, NATO stock numbers and the NATO phonetic alphabet being universal.

As the requirements began to evolve there were changes to the post-war structure of the Air Force and with demobilisation and the drawdown in men and materiel, problems challenged expectations. As noted in Chapter 1, when Tactical Air Command (TAC) was formed on 21 March 1946 it comprised the Third, Ninth and Twelfth Air Forces. For a brief period it also had the Nineteenth Tactical Air Command and Ninth Troop Carrier Command. The latter two commands were deactivated on 31 March and that was necessary to focus operational roles and responsibilities across what was a very different range of capabilities and traditions. The three Air Forces remaining provided an almost perfect balance between capabilities and orientations.

Third Air Force had a great tradition for training and would do the long haul on movements between the Ninth AF on the East Coast and Twelfth AF on the West Coast. But the Ninth AF had a very combat-rich history and would do much to inculcate the entire Command with that ethos. However, the distinct lines of expertise that had characterised their operational record to date could not be maintained and a new dispersal of training and operational deployment was required. While the Command was drawn to get on with its responsibilities it was deflected by the pressing demands of demobilisation and force reductions that also had to cope with decommissioned fields and stations. General Quesada was adamant that 'We must train and we must train a great deal. We are in a horrible state; to put it bluntly, we are in a hell of a state'.

It was impossible to retain a combat-ready force with the mounting problems and Quesada made standardisation of capabilities a priority. Nevertheless the Air Force deactivated Third AF on 1 November and enforced widespread adoption of what became known as the Hobson Plan, whereby wings would

Air-to-air rockets equipped fighter-bomber units and turned interceptors into ground attack aircraft in a role developed widely during the Second World War when these weapons were dubbed the Holy Moses. (USAF)

be organised along functional lines. That was implemented on 27 June 1947 at MacDill AFB, Florida. This reduced the size of the individual units and gave the commanding officer greater familiarity with the personnel and the duties of the men under his command. It also began to implement the Aircraft Maintenance Organization Plan which further consolidated standardisation and prepared TAC for the Directorate System which brought it under the same organisational philosophy as the highest echelons in the Air Force.

With this accomplished, TAC played its part in planning for an Air Force with 55 operational combat groups, under which plan it had to recall 400 reserve officers and increase tactical exercises. These included a hypothetical invasion of the Carolinas and of Alaska, where Arctic conditions would show deficiencies in some of the equipment, including aircraft. For the crews, the operational word was 'jointness' in which all the separate elements contributed. But as planning appeared to be in step with improvements, from 1 December 1948 all TAC units and Air Defense Command (ADC) became operational headquarters under Continental Air Command (ConAC).

While losing its identity, TAC had a specific mission which was to provide 'USAF cooperation with surface forces and operational training'. It already had a mixed force of fighters, fighter-bombers, light and medium bombers and transport aircraft for logistical supply and for moving men and materiel to wherever they might be needed. But there was an important distinction between air support in the Second World War and that of the late 1940s, where operations were now unleashed from Army doctrine and free to exploit air power doctrine.

At the time of its absorption into ConAC, TAC had 31,731 personnel and 1,061 aircraft of which 298 were fighters including 73 F-80 and 69 F-84 jets in 11 wings operating out of 16 bases. On 15–19 March 1948, TAC conducted Exercise Timberline, a mountain operation in which it showed the superiority of F-80s in the ground-attack role over Army divisional artillery against specified targets. It had also played a significant part in Operation Vittles, the supply of food and fuel to beleaguered citizens of Berlin when the Russians threw a blockade on that city, preventing surface transport in or out. In July it had received its first tactical bombers when B-45s arrived with the 47th Bombardment Group and on 23 August 1948 TAC got its first F-84s at Turner AFB, Georgia.

After it had formed on 21 March 1946 with the mission to deliver the atomic bomb on enemy targets in time of war, Strategic Air Command (SAC) was apportioned a lean complement of fighters, one of two fighter groups being equipped with P-51s and a second without any aircraft at all. In this first year, SAC embarked on a major series of operational evaluations and crew familiarisation exercises linked to tests on the effects of atomic weapons, carrying out overflights of European countries looking for airfields which could be of use in time of war. These operations are described in detail in Volume 2.

In 1947, of a total complement of 713 tactical aircraft, SAC boasted 230 P-51 Mustangs and 120 P-80 Shooting Star jet fighters in five fighter groups. In the following year, only 131 Mustangs were on strength along with 81 F-82 Twin Mustang fighters but 1948 was a year of great change in SAC with the introduction of the six-engine B-36 and extensive inflight refuelling capabilities. In 1949 the comparative inventory at SAC favouring bombers over fighters showed only 161 of the latter in a total tactical complement of 868 aircraft, the new F-86 accounting for half of the fighter force. The emphasis on fighter escort diminished with the Very-Heavy-Bomber (VHB) category extending the strike range over intercontinental distances.

High Velocity Aircraft Rocket (HVAR) projectiles fired by an F-86 as post-war jets mirrored the expansion of capabilities. (USAF)

These paper inventories lack detail and context, the actual number of fighter units with SAC fluctuating up and down during the late 1940s. On paper, by the end of 1946 SAC had the 56th FG and the 4th FG but the latter was only manned in March 1947 as personnel began to trickle through. Activated at Selfridge Army Air Field, Michigan, the 56th with its 21 P-47s was assigned to the Fifteenth AF, where it began to convert to P-51s but did not receive the jet-powered P-80 until early 1947. Three new Fighter Groups (27th, 33rd and 82nd) were activated in 1947 with manning beginning somewhat later. In that year, SAC HQ took responsibility for the 4th, the 56th and the 82nd but the 27th and 33rd were quickly assigned to Eighth AF.

The five remaining fighter groups were redesignated as fighter wings in August 1948. But the requirement to reduce down to just two fighter wings for the 70-group Air Force then being sought sent the 4th, 33rd and 56th to ConAC in mid-1949. Pressures on manpower and resources caused it to lose the 82nd there also, reducing its fighter force to just the 27th FW. The drawdown was a reflection of just how quickly the conversion to very-long-range bombers and their capacity for self-defence was effected through the new generation of aircraft emerging in 1948, primarily with the B-36 but also as a result of the increase in inflight refuelling.

Increasingly in the pre-ballistic missile era, the need to protect airfields and bomber bases from air attack sent operational requirements into Arctic spaces, driving the demand for all-weather fighters with specifications met in part by the F-89 Scorpion and the F-94 Starfire. By the end of 1949, SAC fighter strength had been reduced to just the 27th FW and the 1st FW but neither were capable of long-duration missions and they were excluded from war plans which required long-range flights. Nevertheless, various techniques had been developed to rapidly move units from the Zone of the Interior across the Atlantic Ocean to European bases.

Mass flights to Europe had been conducted by making numerous stops en-route and without the need for inflight tankers which were assigned to bombers. The first of these occurred on 16 July 1948 when 16 F-80s from the 56th FG conducted FOX ABLE ONE to the UK and later the 27th FW moved 180 F-84Es from Bergstrom AFB, Texas, to Germany with a smaller migration occurring when 55 F-82s made the trip to the Caribbean. Further exercises demonstrated that by land-hopping it was possible to move tactical fighter units across large areas of the globe, freeing up the tanker force for supporting the bombers.

The Fighter Mentality

Clearly, as discussed in previous chapters, the post-war Air Force both before and after independence in 1947 was dominated by a bomber mentality both in doctrine and in policy. It was one shared by the public and by politicians. The bombers had 'won the war' by knocking out German and Japanese factories, ruined their machinery and marshalling yards and planted chaos on production lines and manufacturing facilities, sending aircraft assembly underground or in caves and tunnels. The fighters had been there to protect the bombers and to knock down defending enemy fighters, playing a secondary-, even if not a minor role. Or so went the public perception.

But the focus had been on destruction and with possession of the atomic bomb, despite demobilisation and deconstruction of the massed military might which created the wartime 'arsenal of democracy', a strategic force capable of destroying an enemy at will was the one the country wanted. And for that the bomber pilots took precedence in command and the rise of the fighter-generals would not occur for the next 20 years. The real value of the fighter during the Second World War had been passed over, largely because the ascendency of the bomber-led command structure ensured greater resources from Congress in a period of defence-spending austerity under the budget axe wielded by the government.

Fighters had enabled the bombers and unleashed their potential by protecting them so that a significant number could reach their targets. They could also destroy the *Luftwaffe*'s defensive fighter forces and their equivalents in the Pacific war. That nuance and context never really engaged because the Air Force wanted the 'big stick' with which to dominate defence spending. And when a generation of bombers emerged to fly independent of the protecting fighters, the escort role diminished with greater emphasis on tactical air support, which is why so many of the new generation jets were required to support fighter, interceptor and ground-attack roles.

While commander of US forces in Europe, General Dwight D Eisenhower had given his blessing to an independent air force only on the basis that priority was given to the bombers while receiving an unequivocal commitment for fighters and fighter-bombers to support ground forces. It was inevitable that projections for requirements in the post-war air force were based on experiences flying and fighting during the Second World War but the comparisons blurred reality. There was a clear distinction between bomber crews and fighter pilots and those would influence decisions and operational doctrine when respective pools of experience were brought to high command.

As discussed previously, selection of air crew allocation depended upon flying skills but it also required an uncertain quotient of psychological profiling of the trainee and not just the natural aptitude for working as a team member or as an individual. The US Army Air Forces had placed greater emphasis on psychological profiling than any other combatant air force of the period, an early definition of the fighting man of the air being set down before America's entry into the war in December 1941. As noted by Roy R Grinker Snr and John P Spiegel in a 1945 report, psychologists noted that flying fighters and bombers:

Require a different sort of person to fly each type successfully. Or rather, the pilot tends to develop a different flying and combat personality when he is exposed to one type of plane or to another. In general, the flying characteristics of heavy, four-engine or two engine bomber type aircraft are those of steadiness, lack of manoeuvrability, reliability and great power over a long distance. Combat missions consume many hours and require considerable persistence and endurance. The fliers in such groups, especially the pilots, tend to fit in with these characteristics. They are usually older, more mature, steadier, and less willing to take risks and indulge in flashy manoeuvers than fighter pilots.

All fighter pilots were required to conduct 300 flying hours on operational missions before allocated a rest period but that required fighter pilots to spend more time exposed to combat than bombers crews because their flight times were much less across a greater number of missions. Four-engine bomber crews were required to conduct 25–35 hours on missions, or 50 missions for twin-engine bombers. But the rate of attrition was appalling. Only 26 percent finished their minimum 25 missions, with four percent lost on each one, the mean average being 14.72 missions completed per crewmember. General Arnold wanted 'individualists with quick agility and facility' to fly fighters and to respond quicker, display high levels of personal motivation and to be able to control aggression unleashed only in the pursuit of their objectives. And the motivation had to be narrowly focused without consideration of survival or failure.

Specific criteria were established for care and recuperation from the stress of combat, rest centres being set up in Atlantic City, New Jersey, or Miami Beach, Florida. Fighter pilots were given special consideration and overseas bases ran on the basis that frequent leave and passes were given along with priority health care and availability of medical facilities for non-combat related consultations. Both fighter pilots and bomber crews were given better prospects for promotion and because of this the command structure was dominated by aircrew rather than ground crew with all the orientations and focus that this implied. Fighter pilots flew more than twice the number of sorties than bomber crews, who nevertheless suffered on average 40 percent more casualties.

The very different reactions to combat gave bomber crews a sense of anxiety, exposed as they were to long hours in cramped, cold and noisy conditions, incessant muscular tension, claustrophobia, frostbite and hypoxia producing a far greater number of immediate and lifelong medical problems than those experienced by fighter pilots. The stress on the bomber crew, where the life of an individual was determined by the action of others, added to a prolonged anticipation of danger ahead resulting in a creeping, cerebral paralysis uncommon in fighter pilots. A far greater number of bomber crew were retired out on medical grounds than their single-seat contemporaries, where psychological stress took a very different form.

The bonds between the man and his machine were in parallel to those between fellow pilots and crewmembers and psychologists concluded that 'the impersonal threat of injury from the enemy, affecting all alike, produces a high degree of cohesion so that personal attachments throughout the unit became intensified. Friendships

Pilot training was challenged by defence budget cuts and by the loss of existing air crew to commercial contracts with airlines, the Air Force recruiting on the basis of a lifelong career rather than a single job. (USAF)

parlous state of fighter units in Strategic Air Command, declining as the bomber inventory grew in capability. In January 1946 General Eisenhower named former bomber chief General Carl A Spaatz as the first Chief of Staff of the Air Force, while acknowledging the role played by pilots of fighters and fighter-bombers who had made the D-Day landings possible and without whose contribution he believed the invasion attempt would have been 'criminal'.

Conditions under which the post-war Air Force had to manage both service and policy requirements and public and political expectations was compromised by the drastic cuts in defence spending, reduced from 41 percent of GDP in 1945 to 4.6 percent in 1948. Yet the domination of the bomber mentality was all-pervasive for aforementioned reasons, and self-sustaining. Major General Perry McCoy has pointed out that 'Bombardment and autonomy were natural partners, but fighters were antithetical to both'.

Any support for a fighter-based doctrine would inevitably have to identify weaknesses with the strategic bombing concept while simultaneously damaging the cause for force autonomy. With the initial task of long-range

are easily made by those who might never have been compatible at home and are cemented under fire'. As eloquently put by Colonel Mike Worden, director of the Chief of Staff's staff-group at USAF headquarters, 'The high price of admission granted them elitism; the high cost of attrition created an unbreakable cohesion'.

During time spent with a fighter squadron in combat, one psychologist observed how the unit had its own value system, representing 'the total social, economic, political, and educational world for the individual member…(Its) status system pervades everything he does, as there is no way to get away from it'. He concluded that fighter pilots were individualistic, highly self-reliant to the point of excluding others, of being 'loners' valuing technical knowledge over general education. He judged that their leaders had 'dependability, standard quick judgment, a "cool head", aggressiveness in the air, and usually superior flying ability… (These) personal qualities of leadership became the criteria for judging men'.

In establishing a leadership cadre for the post-war period it was for two reasons that the bomber force elevated its senior and most experienced officers to command of the new and independent air force. One reason was the publication of the *US Strategic Bombing Survey* which did much to elevate awareness of the remarkable development of that new capability in air warfare. The second reason was the central role of strategic bombing given to the independent, post-war air force, command of which naturally rested with those principally responsible for the development of that capability. There will be much more of that discussed in Volume 2.

There was no equivalent post-war survey of fighter forces or of tactical air support for ground forces and the presence of those elements on the horizon, rather than in the foreground of warfighting doctrine, appeared to some as a mirage without substance A harsh interpretation perhaps but one which could draw as evidence the

escort, the community of fighter pilots and their leaders accepted the doctrinal pre-eminence of the bombers-first policy if only to support autonomy. Because of this the fighter advocates had a hard time lobbying for more attention to their cause, made increasingly difficult by the resources awarded to increasingly more complex and costly bombers but it failed to prevent leaders and commanders from that fraternity from expressing their displeasure.

The priority given to bombers is evident within the command structure and ranking. TAC was commanded by Elwood Quesada, a major general, while SAC was commanded by George C Kenney, a four-star general, while only one of the eight AAF generals with three or more stars was a fighter general. Arthur T Hadley, a somewhat cynical outside observer, concluded that the fighter general had been placed into 'military Siberias far from where the press or Congress could hear the questions they raised'.

The post-war US Air Force was dominated by bomber-generals, 80 percent of whom came from the Pacific war and of those no fewer than 75 percent were from the Twentieth AF flying B-29 missions from the isolated islands in the Pacific Ocean. A tight-knit community of autonomous units operating with very little political or inter-service challenges, they were all under the command of Major General Curtis E LeMay who in 1947 was commander in chief of all USAFE units and would play a major role in orchestrating the Berlin Airlift, returning to command SAC in 1948. Conversely, two-thirds of the senior and three-quarters of the fighter cohort had fought in the skies over Europe and were uniquely qualified in working with the Army and with international allied partners.

Thus were the two fraternities polarised around very different backgrounds. Not until the mid-1960s would the fighter-generals gain ascendency over the bomber-generals, who held sway over prioritised decisions throughout the late 1940s and 1950s.

A Citizen Air Force

A long-standing tradition of American military preparedness is the concept of the 'citizen soldier', dating back to the seventeenth century and defence of the colonies. Based on the unassailable continental frontier of oceans to east and west protected by the Navy and friendly neighbours north and south, citizen soldiers could be mobilised as required to fight enemies as they might emerge. Enshrined within reluctance to accept a standing army of paid soldiery, the United States citizen understood the need to rise from a daily labour, take up arms and defend the nation and its constitution. Or so goes the mantra prevalent in the early decades of the United States after the Declaration of Independence in 1776.

One hundred years later, the complexities of modern warfare and the need for mobilisation to face very different border threats brought a rethink. The requirement for technical expertise and an officer corps to lead willing men in battle became a prerequisite to development of the United States into a modern industrial nation. And when the invention of the aeroplane, and its application to military purposes during the First World War, introduced another layer of technical and operating complexity, the citizen soldier filled a niche as an adjunct to a professional, career-orientated soldiery.

In 1909, the First Aero Company, Signal Corps, New York National Guard came into existence, and in 1940 the National Guard boasted 29 observation squadrons and nearly 4,800 personnel. In 1946, with the formation of the first Air Guard unit the organisational structure was set for the formation of the Air National Guard a year later, concurrent with the independent US Air Force.

The citizen soldier now had wings and could fly. Over time it would take an honourable place alongside the full-time Air Force and provide supplementary support and added resources in time of national need. And all the while, being a local, state-run banner for developing an air-minded youth directed perhaps toward a professional career in the full-time Air Force. But it was not regarded as such by many senior Air Force notaries in the early post-war years.

In February 1944 the AAF had completed its 'Initial Plan for the Post War Air Force' which anticipated a million-man force independent of the Army and bearing the burden of national security with little regard for the Army or the Navy, or in fact for the 'part-time pranksters' in the National Guard. The leadership wanted fully committed airmen, professionally trained for constant levels of readiness and with no lifestyle distractions, seeing these as sapping the energy and the commitment of a truly professional airman. Or as one cynical recruit called it: 'Bootcamp for all'.

The post-war force thus envisaged would have 105 air combat groups, no place for military preparedness or the training of a state-controlled National Guard, where the command structure would be diluted between Washington DC and the responsible officials in each state. Constantly stressing the need for a force-in-being without the paraphernalia of a reserve force 'plucked from the fields and farmlands' of rural America, there was open hostility to a post-war Guard. This was self-evidently unrealistic, ignoring the value in proud and committed men who stood ready to fight for their country, accepting career chances blighted by a call-to-arms in times of crises. There was precedent for this negative viewpoint. Their treatment during the Second World War had been appalling and their contribution ignored by the public relations machine of the AAF.

As the Air Staff looked to the post-war situation, they sustained this negative attitude and recommended that the National Guard be mostly composed of aircraft control and warning units; in British equivalence, this was tantamount to a Royal Observer Corps role. But there were dissident voices proclaiming the value of the Guard, including General Tompkins who on 15 June 1945 testified before the House Select Committee on Postwar Military Policy that it should be considered 'our first line of reserve in an emergency'. Sheer performance during wartime and the reconsidered judgement of senior officers now fully aware of plans for a drastic reduction in the armed services, tipped in favour of the Guard and its retention.

Conforming to the bidding of the Truman administration, General George C Marshall sought to justify his rundown in the armed services in the face of fierce opposition by speaking up for reserve forces and Guard units that could, in a time of crisis, rise to the needs of the nation. It was a classic volte-face of epic proportions but worked in favour of the establishment of the Air National Guard, approved on 15 April 1946 and targeting 30 June 1947 as completion date for its organisation. Under this revised plan, the ANG would be primarily equipped with fighters which were suited due to their small size, minimal support requirements, low maintenance and operational versatility. An added value was that they could be diverted from surplus stock marked out for decommissioning. Thus, despite strong reservations from the AAF, the need for an Air National Guard was forced upon post-war planners by a decimated funding projection, major reductions in men and aircraft and by the need to keep a satisfactory capability.

On 30 June 1946 the Denver 120th FS was the first Air National Guard unit to get formal federal recognition. From 21 August, inactivated AAF designations were transferred to the ANG and redesignated into 20 fighter groups incorporating 62 squadrons, two light bomb groups with four squadrons and five composite groups with 12 fighter squadrons. That made them eligible for surplus aircraft, mostly P-47s and P-51s, with their main role being the defence of the continental United States. By the end of 1949 the ANG had 514 units and a total 2,401 aircraft of which 211 were jet fighters, representing about 10 percent of the total fighter strength in the United States. Personnel strength had risen to 44,728 including 3,600 pilots.

Flight clothing evolved rapidly in the jet era, with the high-speed/high-altitude capabilities of early-generation jets requiring specialised anti-g suits which in the United States were pioneered by Earl H Wood, Charles Code and Edward H Lambert. (USAF)

APPENDIX: STALLED AND TRANSIENT PROJECTS

During the latter stages of the war, manufacturers responded to AAF requests for advanced or speculative concepts and some of these held promise that could have seen operational service had the war gone on longer. Others were unsatisfactory and useful only for demonstrating inadequacies with what turned out to be basically flawed designs or inappropriate concepts. A few are of note for the capability they may have provided if developed to their full potential while others were dubious at best, a product of excessive experimentation over performance.

The period 1942–1949 was an explosive indulgence in a wide range of technical and engineering innovations tried and tested from German, and in some cases Japanese, wartime research. Reaction engines had been used in several German test programmes including pure jet, turbojet or turboprop, in addition to ramjet, solid propellant and liquid propellant rockets. Obsessed with scouring all collated data and exploiting all the research work discovered in German research facilities, US manufacturers seized upon these often highly questionable concepts to procure more business and get government contracts.

While already engaged in a laborious and time-consuming demobilisation programme, the Air Force itself was to a great degree seduced by the sometime false promise of exciting new ideas and impressive demonstrations from one-off tests. But what works well on a testbed, or in a specially designed prototype, may not perform well in operational service and sorting one from the other would support a wide and diverse range of different aircraft types. Which made the period 1945–1949 such a rich harvest in new and exciting ideas for a new and increasingly tense Cold War. Aircraft with different propulsion concepts were frequently visible on airfields and test facilities across the United States as a result of an urgent need to maintain currency with extant technology.

What follows are descriptions of types developed during the Second World War but with some post-war service as interceptors or escort fighters, together with types proposed and flown but not adopted for serial production or operational service. These are listed according to the chronological order of first flight.

Northrop P-61; First Flight: 26 May 1942

An unlikely contender for fighter design, Northrop had produced the first US dedicated night-fighter, the P-61 Black Widow which saw some limited service after the war. The concept arose in 1940 after the British Purchasing Commission expressed a need for a high-altitude, high-speed night-fighter to attack incoming *Luftwaffe* bomber formations. When the British Technical Mission went to the United States and shared UK radar secrets with the Americans the requirement was passed along by Lieutenant General Delos C Emmons, who encouraged US industry to marry an air-intercept radar with a suitable platform in the hope of gaining an order from the British. Radar was very new to aircraft interception (AI) but work was already underway to provide an airborne AI system which would, with the weight of the equipment required, necessitate a large, twin-engine aircraft.

At the time, engine contenders included the Pratt & Whitney 2800 Double Wasp and the Wright R-3350 Duplex Cyclone, both radials which could produce more than 2,000hp (1,500kW). Wright Field's Air Technical Service Command evaluated the concept and concluded that it would be possible to produce such a capability through an aircraft with a loiter time of up to eight hours, extremely long for 1940. Moreover, it would require sufficient firepower to bring down large bombers. Accordingly, specifications for such an aircraft were drawn up and discussed with the then US Army Air Corps and on 5 November 1940 Northrop submitted a proposal,

An Air Defense Command Northrop P-61B-20-NO (43-8279) operated by the 318th FS at Hamilton Field, California in December 1947. (USAF)

winning out against the Douglas XA-26A, an adaptation of the A-26 attack aircraft.

Initially, the design incorporated an extended fuselage nacelle housing AI radar, two gun-turrets, a three-man crew and fuel tanks, twin radial engines and twin tail booms with the aircraft supported on a tricycle landing gear. The design adopted a unique form of wing flap designed by Edward Zaparka to increase both lift and drag characteristics, operating as a split flap with the lower portion sliding aft on tracks and hinging down as it moved rearward. This increased both wing camber and the effective surface area. When Northrop presented its design there were critics, unable to envisage a fighter with a weight of 22,600lb (10,251kg) and of such size powered by two Double Wasp engines.

The definitive design was submitted to Air Materiel Command on 5 December and a procurement decision verified 12 days later with a contract awarded for two prototypes. A full-scale mock-up was examined on 2 April 1941 and several technical and a few design changes were requested, including the relocation of four 20mm M2 cannon from the outer wings to the under-fuselage position allowing more fuel and better lift characteristics for the wings. Changes were also forthcoming in the design of the dorsal turret and the option of underwing drop tanks was incorporated. Several design innovations included smaller ailerons with wider span flap, which allowed a very low landing speed, and the use of spoilerons, spoilers which could be operated asymmetrically for added roll control at both high and low speeds.

A Western Electric SCR-70A radar was installed in the nose with a typical 'greenhouse' cockpit at two levels, a lower position for the pilot and a slightly higher position for the gunner behind, who was seated slightly above the level of the pilot. The radar operator was located in the aft fuselage enclosure facing forward where he could operate the AI equipment, a homing device and the navigations sets. With a range of almost 5 miles (8km), the SCR-720A supplemented a link to the pilot enabling him to steer on to the detected target using voice commands after which the pilot would use a smaller screen to close in. The dorsal turret would be operated by the gunner or by the radar operator with a full 360 degree rotation and 90 degrees in elevation. The fuselage had a total length of 33.8ft (10.3m), against a total length of 49.5ft (15m) and a wingspan of 66ft (20.1m).

The 348th Night Fighter Squadron (NFS) was formed at Orlando Army Air Base, Florida, in October 1942 with personnel who had been trained by the Royal Air Force on night interception operations. An initial complement of Douglas DB-70 Havocs were replaced with the YP-61 Black Widow in September 1943 and training courses prepared crew and aircraft for the European theatre. The 422nd NFS moved to England in February 1944, followed by the 425th aboard the *Queen Elizabeth*, adapted for troop transport and related war work. The 422nd received its first aircraft that June and within a month began operations over England with the first engagement being against a V1 flying bomb on 15 July, but the rear fuselage cone imploded and the attack was called off.

Deployed variously to airfields in France in August 1944 and then Belgium, the 422nd had some successes. Generally, it was judged that the P-61 was too slow to effectively accomplish its design role and considerable field adaptations were made, frequently deleting turrets and gunners but retaining the radar operator in the back. Operations in the Mediterranean theatre came too late to have any measurable record against the enemy and the 6th NFS received its P-61s for the Pacific theatre in June 1944. Operations were compromised by the late arrival of drop tanks, which would have been useful in getting crews back safely through enemy skies, at night and frequently with damage.

The P-61 was useful in its role but arrived too late to make a noticeable impression and had not been fully bedded-in when the war ended. Nevertheless, with 706 produced, the aircraft was operated by all three combat commands and would remain in service until 1954, USAFE equipping its night-fighter force with the P-61 from bases in Germany and Austria with some units interchanging the de Havilland Mosquito. In the Pacific region, several squadrons were inactivated while others were integrated with occupation forces in Japan as others with long flying hours parted out and were disassembled on Luzon.

In the United States, all three combat commands employed the Black Widow and several were used for special development tests, their high load-carrying capability for aircraft of this type being especially beneficial for tests with ejection seats. Again, German research had advanced the art of escaping a stricken aircraft with an ejection system tested by Helmut Schenk in a Heinkel He-280 jet fighter on 13 January 1942. With iced-up controls he successfully ejected during a test of the Argus As 014 pulse-jet for the V1 flying bomb. The Heinkel He-219 Uhu fighter, produced from 1942, was the first aircraft to fly with an ejection system designed in. This research was used by the AAF to conduct tests with a converted P-61 redesignated XP-61B and on 17 April 1946, First Sergeant Lawrence Lambert became the first American to eject, travelling at 302mph (486km/hr) at 7,800ft (2,380m). It was this activity that began the use of ejection seats in new aircraft.

The P-61 was also utilised for flights on the Thunderstorm Project which involved US Navy and NACA participation for a research effort conducted between 1946 and 1949 carrying science instruments for measurements to provide detailed data for the US Weather Bureau. Remarkably, information thus obtained has remained the core science for current studies into high-energy weather systems and thunderstorm science.

In other operations, the US Navy borrowed two P-61s for tests with the Martin Gorgon IV ramjet missile and the first launch occurred on 14 November 1947, the two Black Widows being returned to the USAF the following year. An RP-61C (45-59300) was used by the NACA from 1948 to 1953 for a series of drop-tests with unmanned aerial vehicles (UAVs) with a second aircraft (43-8330) from 1950 and a third (42-39754) used for ramjet tests, retired on 9 August 1954.

Table 8: Northrop P-61 Specifications

	XP-61	P-61A	P-61B	P-61C
Span	66ft/20.11m	66ft/20.11m	66ft/20.11m	66ft/20.11m
Length	48.83ft/14.88m	48.83ft/14.88m	49.58ft/15.11m	49.58ft/15.11m
Height	14.16ft/4.31m	14.16ft/4.31m	14.66ft/4.47m	14.66ft/4.47m
Empty weight	19,245lb/8,730m	20,965lb/9,510kg	22,000lb/9,979kg	24,000lb/10,886kg
Gross weight	25,150lb/11,408kg	27,700lb/12,565kg	29,700lb/13,472kg	30,600lb/13,880kg
Max speed	370mph/595kph	372mph/599kph	366mph/589kph	430mph/692kph
Ceiling	33,100ft/10,089m	34,000ft/10,363m	33,100ft/10,089m	41,000ft/12,497m
Range	1,200mls/1,931km	1,210mls/1,947km	1,010mls/1,625km	1,000mls/1,609km

Northrop XP-59; First flight: 30 September 1943

One of the more speculative projects of the wartime period was the tailless Northrop XP-79 which originated as a rocket-powered, high-speed interceptor but was later equipped with two Westinghouse 19-B turbojet engines for flight tests and redesignated XP-79B. The concept followed Jack Northrop's advocacy of the tailless flying-wing configuration which was far ahead of its time but lacking the automated stabilisation and control systems that only advanced electronic flight control equipment could provide. But Jack Northrop was convinced that a clean, flying wing concept would provide efficiency, performance and a broader range of mission roles than could be provided with conventional configurations of fuselage, wings and tail.

On 15 September 1942 Jack Northrop had presented his 'Jet-Driven Interceptor' design to the AAF as a tailless flying wing aircraft powered by a rocket motor with the pilot prone in the nose of the machine so that he could better withstand high g-forces. This would also allow the cockpit area to be smaller than required for a seated pilot. The proposal was extensive and well substantiated as a joint venture with the Daniel Guggenheim School of Aeronautics at the California Institute of Technology (GALCIT) and the Aerojet Corporation. Both organisations were already working with the AAF on both liquid and solid boost-assisted take-off propulsion. The AAF liked the concept and decided that AMC would conduct most of the work as Northrop was already busy with existing work on the N-9, a precursor to the XB-35 flying wing bomber.

Designated XP-79, the concept was radical and the AMC decided to build a flying mock-up to test it and incorporate any desirable changes into the prototype. That was modified into a contract for three experimental gliders built primarily of wood by AMC at Wright Field under research programme MX-324 and work started on 1 November 1942. The project was classified Top Secret as was all activity on the flying wing concept including the N-9 and the XB-35. The XP-79 began life with Northrop already busy with another tailless project, albeit not a flying wing configuration.

Northrop's flying wing research for the Army began in response to Circular Proposal R-40C on 27 November 1939 for a high-speed fighter and three companies responded, receiving a contract for the tailless XP-56 on 22 June 1940. The first prototype was still in assembly when work started on the XP-79, its flight delayed due to problems finding a suitable engine. Eventually equipped with a 2,000hp (1,492kW) Pratt and Whitney R-2800-29 radial engine in the back of the fuselage nacelle, it would make its first flight on 30 September 1943. Northrop and the AMC learned a lot about flying wing design, handling and performance which fed in to the XB-35.

Meanwhile, Northrop started work on the MX-324 gliders and on a follow-on contract for three XP-79 rocket propelled interceptor prototypes under MX-325. In this, the three gliders would serve as engineering development precursors to the XP-79 as the N-9 was to the XB-35. In order to loosen the constraints on classification, the unpowered gliders would come under MX-334 and received a Confidential category.

The three gliders were of welded steel tubing for the centre-sections with wood outer wing panels over wood interior members. Two landing skids were provided together with elevons controlled through the rudder bar. The gliders had unusually high stress levels of +/- 18g and early analysis indicated that a vertical tail would be necessary for high-speed flight. Much to Northrop's disgust, the chief aerodynamicist Dr William R Sears devised a wooden, wire-braced vertical tail which could be removed should flight trials indicate it was unnecessary. Jack Northrop was alloyed to the idea of a flying wing devoid of any projecting control surfaces. The first glider was completed by late spring of 1943 and shipped to the NACA's Langley Laboratory for wind tunnel tests but it would not get into the air until later that year.

Delivered in late August to the Mojave Desert, the second glider was first towed captive behind a Cadillac but oscillations and porpoising prevented it getting airborne until a four-wheel dolly was attached and a tethered flight achieved on 4 September with Harry Crosby at the controls. To achieve proper independent flight, a P-38 was modified for towing and on 1 October 1943 it momentarily left the ground, a more effective flight taking place the next day with test pilot John Myers in the cramped cockpit. Northrop got the XP-56 into the air for the first time on 6 September and before the end of the month would get good drag data from the N-9M while on 9 November 1943 the first flight of the third MX-334 glider took place. It crashed the following day when Crosby, unable to recover from a stall when it became inverted, took to his parachute.

Back from Langley, the No 1 glider made its first flight on 30 November and would support the No 2 glider, which would be responsible for most of the trials from this date. Several modifications were carried out as results came in, including the addition of a tricycle undercarriage. By early 1944 the No 2 glider had been modified to accept the Aerojet XCAL-200 rocket motor with a thrust of 200lb (890N), propellant tanks carrying mono ethyl aniline fuel and red fuming nitric oxide oxidiser on either side of the pilot who was notionally protected by neoprene curtains. It was with this engine installed that the project reverted to MX-324.

Tests with the engine installed were carried out on 20 June at Harper Dry Lake and on 5 July 1944 Crosby conducted the first US rocket-powered aircraft flight after release from the P-38 over the lakebed near Barstow, California. Further flights followed, the last on 1 August 1944 after which the two surviving MX-334/MX-324 aircraft were delivered to Air Technical Service Command at Wright Field. For some time, one was displayed at Wright Field as an outdoors display item but both were scrapped in 1949. Immediately after flight tests with the test aircraft, all attention turned quickly to the XP-79 under MX-365.

The plan was to build three XP-79 aircraft powered by the 2,000lb (8.9kN) thrust Aerojet XCAL-2000 rocket motor which was believed to provide it with a top speed of 538mph (865km/hr) based on a consumption of 5.17lb (2.34kg) per second for a total propellant load of 8,400lb (3,810kg). Like the XP-56 the XP-79 would primarily use magnesium in construction and this, together with

A P-59A Airacomet preserved at March Field Air Museum. (Peter Stroobach)

the propellants, could cause the entire aircraft to quickly become a flaming incendiary if hit during combat. Steel armour plate was used to provide some degree of protection but there were many concerns over the aircraft's vulnerability.

Due to existing contracts and other development work, Northrop subcontracted the design and construction of the three aircraft to Avion, which had just formed near Maywood, California. But the rocket engine ran into development problems and on 27 April 1943 authorisation was received to replace it with two 1,150lb (5.1kN) thrust Westinghouse 19-B axial-flow J30 jet engines with the re-designation XP-79B, replacing an earlier derivation using a less powerful engine and designated XP-79A. Northrop felt so confident in their programme that they unsuccessfully requested a contract for 13 YP-79A and B types. But problems were encountered throughout these preparations and, with the war considered to be in its final stages, in September 1944 the two XP-79s were cancelled, leaving only the jet-powered XP-79B.

A small company with fewer than 100 employees, Avion ran into problems and on 1 December 1944 the sole airframe was moved back to Northrop where work to completion began. A full inspection was held on 29 May 1945 but with no chance of production only issues of pilot safety were marked up for attention. With the two Westinghouse turbojet engines installed, the aircraft was trucked to Muroc where taxi tests were conducted before high-speed runs began on 13 July. To circumvent a problem with the single nose wheel, two smaller wheels were attached just outboard of the two engines nestled against the cockpit and two larger wheels aft, all four of which would fold up into the wing. In flight, the pilot was expected to encounter up to 12g.

Overall, the XP-79A was small, with a total length of 14ft (4.26m) and a wingspan of 38ft (11.58m). It would have carried four .5-in cannon as armament but there was a secondary function to its role. Pilots involved with the programme claimed that its high speed and reinforced wing leading-edge would have allowed it to survive a slicing impact with the outer wing or horizontal tail of an enemy aircraft. This claim has never been seen in print and may be a myth arising from debate among combat crews of similar slash-attacks being conducted by German and Japanese pilots toward the end of the war. As it was, when the XP-79B took to the sky for the first time on 12 September 1945 it was to be its last, the pilot, Harry Crosby, losing control and crashing.

To say that this aircraft was novel is a serious understatement. It had no conventional flight control surfaces, with air intakes at each wing tip replacing ailerons for lateral control operating split elevons opening differentially and for roll and pitch control. Additional yaw control was provided by airbrakes located outboard of the air intakes in a configuration which would be applied to the YB-49 and the X-35 prototype bombers, the B-2 of the 1980s and the B-21 of the 2020s. The programme is worthy of an important place in the annals of unusual aircraft in that it was not a dead-end, as were so many in this period, but rather an idea far ahead of its time.

Table 9: Northrop XP-59 Specifications

	XP-59
Span	45.5ft,13.87m
Length	38.16ft/11.63m
Height	12.33ft/3.76m
Empty weight	7,940lb/3,600kg
Gross weight	12,700lb/5,760kg
Max speed	413mph/664kph
Ceiling	46,200ft/14,080m
Range	240mls/386km

Convair XP-81; First Flight: 11 February 1945

Consolidated merged with Vultee Aircraft in March 1943 and would be known colloquially as Convair, famous for a range of aircraft including the B-36 intercontinental strategic bomber and several jet fighters in the F-102 and F-106 series during the 1950s and 1960s. It also produced the 880 and 990 airliners. Convair was acquired by General Dynamics in 1953 before it was sold on to McDonnell Douglas in 1994. Convair had a prodigious research division and proposed several unusual concepts and was eager to produce combat aircraft for the new jet age. But the limited capabilities of the jet engine stimulated alternatives which made optimum use of both reaction and reciprocating forms of propulsion.

In 1943 the AAF was examining the possibility of providing separate turboprop and jet engines in a new long-range escort fighter to serve the requirements of the Pacific theatre. The requirement was demanding, a range of 1,250 miles (1,930km) and a maximum speed of 500mph (804km/hr). Working with the AAF on concept development, Convair's Model 102 was designated XP-81 when two prototypes (44-91000 and 44-91001) were ordered on 11 February 1944 as a hybrid escort fighter utilising the turboprop engine for cruise and the turbojet for high-speed work. Much analysis had been conducted by the NACA and the AAF into the optimum use of jet engines and the turboprop was showing distinct advantages, particularly with fuel efficiency.

In the interests of supporting what was perceived to be an urgent demand for a long-range escort, and with the war in Europe projected to free up men and materiel for the assault on Japan, a further 13 YP-81s were ordered, powered by the XT31-GE-1 turboprop promising a thrust of 2,300hp (2,715kW) and a General Electric J33-GE-5 turbojet engine with a thrust of 3,750lb (16.68kN). Development of the aircraft, which would have had six nose guns, stalled when the turboprop engine encountered difficulties and was replaced on the first prototype with a Packard Merlin V-1560-7 engine scavenged from a P-51D, with a P-38J radiator intake below the spinner.

Some changes had to be made to compensate for the shift in the centre of gravity and the first flight on 11 February 1945 demonstrated good performance improved stability through the use of a rounded fin extension and the addition of a second, ventral fin. Progress with the development of the XP-81 was rapid and there were plans to greatly expand the production lot but progress with the war in the Pacific led to cancellation of the entire programme

Propelled by a dual propulsion system incorporating turboprop and turbojet engines, the XP-81 was a novel attempt to provide the AAF with a long-range escort fighter. (USAF)

just before VJ Day. Work went ahead with installing the XT31-GE-1 engine in the first prototype and the first flight by an American aircraft with a turboprop engine took place on 21 December 1945.

It was clear from the flight trials that the overall performance of the aircraft was not appreciably greater than the P-51D and development of this engine was cancelled on 9 May 1947. Redesignated ZXF-81 indicating testbed category, the following year both prototypes found space on the bombing range at Edwards AFB and from there they went to the USAF museum.

Table 10: Convair XP-81

	XP-81
Span	50.5/15.39m
Length	44.83ft/13.67m
Height	14.0ft/4.27m
Empty weight	12,755lb/5,786kg
Gross weight	19,500lb/8,850kg
Max speed	507mph/811kph
Ceiling	36,500ft/10,800m
Range	2,500mls/4,022km

Bell XP-83; First Flight: 25 February 1945
Bell had also produced the XP-83, a heavy escort fighter which began in March 1943 as their Model 40, first as an interceptor before the AAF changed the requirement a month later. Bell based the design on the general layout of the Airacomet because that appeared optimum for keeping the fuselage free for maximum fuel load and payload. With an empty weight of 14,105lb (6,398kg), it was almost twice as heavy as the 7,940lb (3,600kg) XP-59. With a full internal fuel load supplemented by two drop tanks, it was estimated to have a range of 1,730 miles (2,784km) and a maximum speed of 522mph (840km/hr). Two prototypes were ordered on 21 July 1944 (44-84990 and 42-84990).

Powered by two XJ33 turbojet engines which had been developed from the J31, each delivering a thrust of 4,000lb (18.0kN), test pilot Jack Woolams made its first flight on 25 February 1945. Like several other jet fighters of its era, the XP-83 suffered from low power and excess weight. It had the unsavoury tendency to buckle the tailplane skin as it ran up on the ground and was judged inadequate for the design task. The second aircraft took to the air on 19 October but it offered too little and was too late, especially as the P-80 Shooting Star was already in Italy on service trials. It ended up on gunnery trials at Wright Field, Ohio.

Table 11: Bell XP-83 Specifications

	XP-83
Span	53.0ft/16.15m
Length	44.83ft/13.67m
Height	15.25ft/4.65m
Empty weight	14,105lb/6,398kg
Gross weight	24,090lb/10,930kg
Max speed	522mph/840kph
Ceiling	45,000ft/13,716m
Range	1,730mls/2,785km

Convair XF-92; First Flight: 18 September 1947
In May 1946 the AAF awarded a contract to Convair for a ramjet-powered interceptor designed to a requirement issued in August 1945 for an aircraft capable of reaching an altitude of 50,000ft (15,240m) in four minutes and a maximum speed of 700mph (1,100km/hr). Several companies had submitted proposals but Convair chose a pure delta with a leading-edge sweep of 60 degrees. The project was covered under MX-813 with the publicly declared designation of XF-92. The delta wing had not been the first profile of choice but consultation with Dr Alexander Lippisch, the famous German designer who had produced a series of delta-wing planforms for research projects in wartime Germany, was already in the United States and on hand for consultation and it was adopted.

Wind tunnel tests verified the aerodynamic advantage of a twin-triangle approach: the larger one for the wing planform itself with the smaller one to profile the vertical tail set 90 degrees to the wing. A nose intake would feed air to a single 1,560lb (6.9kN) Westinghouse J30-WE-1 turbojet engine supplemented by six 2,000lb (8.89kN) thrust rocket motors. Both configuration and propulsion were chosen for the underpinning requirement for a point defence interceptor with outright performance ahead of range and endurance.

The concept envisaged was for an air defence system for which, only a few years hence, guided missiles and anti-aircraft rockets would find a role. The AAF considered the XF-92 more a concept-evaluation programme than a contender for series production and urged rapid development to flight tests needed to achieve early full analysis of its potential. Accordingly, Convair's Model 7-002 (46-682) used parts from existing aircraft to speed final design and assembly. The landing gear came from the North American FJ-1 Fury, the nose wheel assembly from the Bell P-63 Kingcobra, the engine and the hydraulics from the Lockheed P-80 Shooting Star while the cockpit canopy and the ejection seat came from the company's own XP-81.

Work that began at Vultee Field, Downey, California, in mid-1947 was moved to the plant in San Diego when that facility was handed over to North American. With ground testing completed before the end of the year it was moved to the NACA's Ames Aeronautical Laboratory for wind tunnel evaluation. Back at San Diego, it was fitted with an Allison J33-A-21 turbojet engine

One of several attempts to provide a long-range escort fighter, the Bell XP-83 was overweight and eclipsed by superior contemporaries. (USAF)

with a rated thrust of 4,250lb (19.9kN), an improvement on the planned J30, and then delivered to Muroc in April 1948. There, it was fitted with the 5,200lb (23.12kN) J33-A-23. Following ground tests and speed runs, a modest hop into the air took place on 9 June 1948 followed by its first proper flight on 18 September.

By this time the project had been deemed redundant to need and consigned to an experimental programme whereby it was redesignated XF-92A prior to further flight tests. Convair test pilots Ellis Shannon and Bill Martin shared the cockpit in turn and completed Phase I contractor trials on 26 August 1949. The Air Force knew it had something in this delta-wing configuration and wanted as much data as possible with which to work up future options. The NACA too was keen to follow flight trials. Phase II testing was undertaken by Air Force test pilots Chuck Yeager and Frank Everest, who found it to have good handling and landing characteristics – one of the big questions with delta-wing aircraft – and exceptional stability up to Mach 0.92.

In 1951, the XF-92A was fitted with a new and more powerful Allison J33-A-29 delivering a thrust of 7,500lb (33.36kN) and made its first flight with this engine on 20 July 1951 piloted by Yeager. There was no noticeable difference in performance but the additional maintenance work required with this engine limited flights to 21 over the next 18 months. Handed over to the NACA in February 1953, on 9 April NACA test pilot Scott Crossfield took it into the air for the first time with a J33-A-16 engine installed delivering a thrust of 8,400lb (37.4kN).

In 23 flights completed by 14 October 1953, Crossfield found it to be highly unstable, necessitating the installation of wing fences. The first 13 NACA flights focused on acquiring data on static longitudinal stability, on dynamic stability, directional control and low-speed handling. A further 10 flights tested various wing fence configurations, the first six below Mach 1 and the last four evaluating low-speed lateral and directional control but during these some of the fences buckled. The fences were removed altogether but on 14 October 1953 the nose wheel buckled during a high-speed taxi run and the aircraft suffered damage, after which it was retired and the programme was closed.

The XF-92A contributed a large amount of data and valuable information about delta-wing aircraft and their handling characteristics. It had provided the Air Force with confidence to move ahead with requirements and specifications for an advanced fighter for the 1950s which will be described in Volume 4. There, the evolution of the F-102 and the F-106, together with the incorporation of area-rule created a generation of fighters capable of maximising the requirements for the post-Korean War period. As such, the XF-92A was progenitor to a new age in aircraft design and layout.

America's first delta-wing aircraft, the XF-92 emerged from an idea promulgated by Dr Alexander Lippisch but was more a concept-demonstrator than a serious attempt at a high-speed interceptor. (USAF)

Table 12: Convair XF-92 Specifications

	XF-92
Span	31.33ft/9.55m
Length	42.5ft/12.99m
Height	17.66ft/5.37m
Empty weight	9,078lb/4,118kg
Gross weight	14,608lb/6,626kg
Max speed	718mph/1,160kph
Ceiling	50,750ft/15,450m

Curtiss-Wright XP-87; First Flight: 5 March 1948

On 26 August 1945 the AAF issued a requirement for a successor to the P-61 which stipulated two engines and six guns and in a revision dated 23 November it set the required maximum speed at 530mph (853km/hr). The following month the requirement was updated to stipulate the use of jet engines, a specification for which Bell, Convair, Douglas, Goodyear, Northrop and Curtiss-Wright submitted proposals. Under the company tag of Model 29A and the service designation XP-87 Blackjack, the Curtiss-Wright company began development of its first all-jet aircraft but it would be the last the company would build before it ceased to function as an independent business, most of its assets going to North American Aviation.

The concept originated as a solution to vulnerable bombers attacking Nazi-occupied Europe from bases in the United States had the British Isles fallen to occupation by German forces. It was also in response to US government doubts about the survivability of the UK as a base for American bombers and that concern was in line with plans to develop the B-36 as an intercontinental bomber. Equivalent in size to a B-25 Mitchell, the sheer size of the XP-71 and the scale of its development programme raised doubts and the programme was cancelled in early 1942 before assembly of the prototypes was complete. By that time the United States was planning a major bombing offensive from British airfields and the requirement had gone.

The last major project proposed by Curtiss-Wright, the XP-71 was conceived as a very heavy long-range escort fighter with two

The Curtiss XP-87 was designed as a successor to the P-61 but failed when it was cancelled in favour of the F-89 Scorpion. (USAF)

prototypes ordered in November 1941. It would have been powered by two turbocharged 3,450hp (2,570kW) Pratt & Whitney R-4360 Wasp Major radial engines driving pusher-propellers, each located inboard of a high-set wing. With a length of 61.9ft (18.8m) and a wingspan of 82.25ft (25m), it would have had an empty weight of 31,060lb (14,089kg) and a projected top speed of 428mph (689km/hr) with a maximum range of 3,000miles (4,800km). Armament would have comprised a 75mm and one 37mm cannon.

A large aircraft, the XP-87 was powered by four Westinghouse XJ34-WE-7 turbojet engines in pairs within a common nacelle under each inner wing position. The first flight occurred on 5 March 1948 and although slower than expected it returned good reports from tests. The USAF ordered 57 fighters and 30 of a reconnaissance variant and to improve performance existing engines were to be replaced with the J47. But optimism was short-lived as the F-89 Scorpion was considered superior and on 10 October 1948 the Blackjack contract was cancelled.

So ended one of the most important names in the early development of American aviation, combining Curtiss and Wright, names which are legendary in aeronautical history. The post-war demise of the company, which had formed on 5 July 1929 from 12 separate manufacturers to become the largest aircraft company in the United States resulted from a lack of design initiative. From a range of US interwar fighters bearing the 'Hawk' name, the last fighter produced by Curtiss-Wright had been the P-60, a development of the P-40 Warhawk and first flown in September 1941. Lacking performance and potential only six were built, although the programme stumbled along with a range of P-60 variants until it was cancelled in June 1943.

Although we have no Curtiss-Wright aircraft to place in the period covered by this book, note should be made of the 14,000 P-40s produced, the 29,269 airframes and 142,840 engines manufactured during the Second World War together with 146,468 electric propellers. From an innovative and successful aircraft design company, Curtiss-Wright spent most of the war manufacturing the products of other companies and failed to maintain investment in new technologies. The company survives today as an ancillary manufacturer supporting a wide range of defence, energy and commercial markets.

Table 13: Curtiss-Wright XP-87 Specifications

	XP-87
Span	60ft/18.28m
Length	62.83ft/19.15m
Height	20ft/6.09m
Empty weight	25,930lb/11,762kg
Take-off weight	49,900lb/22,635kg
Max speed	600mph/966kph
Ceiling	41,000ft/12,497m

McDonnell XF-85 Goblin; First Flight: 23 August 1948

With immediate post-war emphasis on massed bomber formations, and a hard-won lesson from the Second World War that bombers could only survive when escorted by long-range fighters, the advent of the jet age brought its own collateral problem: how could a fuel-hungry fighter compromised on duration ever provide the necessary cover on intercontinental flights? By mid-1942 plans for a post-war Air Force prompted concerns when it became apparent that jet engines would supplant the piston-engine for high-speed combat aircraft. Geographically isolated from potential enemies, the fighter role was prioritised around protecting the bombers.

The AAF had put tremendous effort into its demand for long-range escort duties supporting the massed armadas of B-17s and B-24s and found a solution with later marks of the P-47 and P-51 which, with aerodynamic refinements and drop tanks, achieved the range to accompany the bombers all the way from England to Berlin and back. In the Pacific theatre, the B-29 had its own concentrated armament and survived against enemy fighter forces protecting Japan while the lessons of the European theatre became entrenched. But escorting bombers across intercontinental distances and through denied airspace would be altogether different.

The evolution to what would become the XF-85 Goblin began with a requirement dated January 1944 and the Air Technical Service Command call for a diminutive piston-engine fighter with a view to it being applied as a parasitic aircraft. Such concepts had been tried before, the first during the First World War and several during the 1930s but none had been successful. Nevertheless, with very long-range missions anticipated for the prospective B-35 and B-36, attention focused on the B-29 as the carrier. Options included small fighters attached to the wingtips of the bomber, underslung from the lower fuselage for release off a trapeze to a system whereby the fighter was buried within the fuselage of the bomber and likewise deployed on a trapeze.

The AAF restructured the requirement in January 1945 for internal carriage in the host aircraft, so as to reduce drag from a protruding airframe, stipulating the use of a jet engine in the fighter, all encompassed in a research programme designated MX-472. While the B-29 remained the prime carrier of choice the far greater range of the B-35 and the B-36, both candidates for full-scale production, enhanced the potential value of an effective and reliable programme. By 1945 the propeller-driven B-36 was in full-scale development and the jet-powered XB-35 was being assembled, but with no certainty as to its future prior to flight tests.

Only McDonnell bid on the request for proposals and on 19 March 1945 a team led by Herman D Barkey submitted their Model 27D. It was a radical design for a bizarre concept, comprising an egg-shaped structure to which were attached 37 degree swept wings, folding vertically until dropped for free flight, three vertical stabilisers and two horizontal stabilisers with dihedral. Propulsion was provided by a single 3,000lb (13.3kN) Westinghouse J34-WE-22 and with sufficient fuel for a flight of 30 minutes. Four .5-in machine guns could be carried in the nose.

Despite the post-conflict embargo on new production orders, the AAF awarded a contract to McDonnell on 9 October for two XF-85 Goblin prototypes (46-523 and 46-524) together with a static test airframe. The mock-up was inspected on 10–12 June 1946 and on

Designed as an experimental parasitic fighter for protecting heavy bombers in denied airspace, the McDonnell XF-85 was never adopted and the concept became redundant with an all-jet bomber force. (USAF)

passing scrutineering the company was awarded a formal Letter of Intent with a concurrent stipulation to Convair that all B-36s from the 24th production B model must have provision for carrying the parasitic fighter. A batch of 30 production Goblins was planned, confirmation pending satisfactory flight trials. It was an option that some B-36Bs would carry three fighters and no bombs. Within a few weeks, that requirement was rescinded and a production plan abandoned.

The Goblin would be restrained by a nose hook attached to an extended portion of the bomber's underslung trapeze for the parasite to fly off and back on again without landing, although a retractable steel skid was provided for an emergency recovery on the ground. The Goblin was expected to display a top speed of 648mph (1,043km/hr) and use its limited operating range to fend off enemy fighters, although there was no specific plan to refuel the aircraft so that it could fly a second time. In examining the operating plan, some AAF pilots doubted the viability of the concept and queried the advisability of reducing the bomb load for such a limited capability.

Flight trials were assigned to a specially modified EB-29B (44-84111) but the first aircraft was damaged on arriving at the NACA's Ames Aeronautical Laboratory for wind tunnel tests so it fell to the second aircraft to conduct three captive flights from 22 July 1948. The first free flight was flown by Edwin Schoch on 23 August from 20,000ft (6,096m) above Muroc Dry Lake. Snatched by violent turbulence on the underside of the EB-29B, the Goblin smashed into the trapeze, shattering the canopy and the pilot's helmet and goggles before dropping down for an emergency landing. Repaired, it conducted three further tests on 14 and 15 October 1948 but on the next flight turbulence again prompted an emergency lakebed landing. The same fate awaited the first aircraft when it made its one and only flight on 8 April 1949, demonstrating that the concept was far too troublesome and the programme was cancelled on 24 October 1949.

Ironically, in flight tests, the XF-85 demonstrated a unique agility and in simulated combat proved very difficult to shoot down. The Goblin programme had endured for five years and demonstrated the persistence of the AAF in trying to find a solution to the problem of the vulnerable bomber, although most of the programme personnel were well aware that it was too fascinating a research opportunity to retire it prematurely. The parasitic role would be reinvented for the FICON (Fighter Conveyor) programme described in Volume 4, gifting the B-36 with another parasitic fighter concept, although that one was driven by the photo-reconnaissance role.

Table 14: McDonnell XF-85 Goblin

	XF-85
Span	21.08ft/6.42m
Length	14.83ft/4.52m
Height	8.25ft/2.51m
Empty weight	3,740lb/1,696kg
Gross weight	4,550lb/2,063kg
Max speed	664mph/1,068kph
Ceiling	48,000ft/14,630m

McDonnell XF-88 Voodoo; First Flight: 20 October 1948

By December 1945 the AAF had decided that it wanted an all-jet combat force of fighters and bombers to replace successful generations of propeller-driven types. The requirement for the XF-88 arose from experience with the P-51D Mustang as a long-range escort fighter for bombers over Germany and on 1 April 1946 McDonnell began work on its Model 36 for a pure-jet successor to that aircraft. Designated XP/XF-88 Voodoo, it bears a name not to be confused with the later and more successful aircraft of a similar name, the F-101 Voodoo which was developed out of the XF-88 when in 1950 the Air Force wanted a replacement for the F-84, outclassed by the Russian MiG fighters in the Korean War.

For power, initially McDonnell focused on the Westinghouse J34-WE-13 turbojet engines with a thrust of 3,000lb (13.3kN) and put two in the wing roots to minimise asymmetric thrust should one fail but they were relocated to outer locations in the lower fuselage with intakes in the wing roots and exhausts on the underside of the rear fuselage which allowed additional fuel for the long-range mission.

This would be the same configuration as that eventually adopted for the F3H Demon and F4 Phantom II of the late 1940s and early 1950s, respectively. For the XF-88, however, initially McDonnell wanted a V-tail in an attempt to reduce the effects of compressibility at high-subsonic speeds. There were to be dive brakes in the aft fuselage and a forward cockpit above the nose which would incorporate six 20mm cannon.

McDonnell received approval to proceed on 7 May 1946 with a contract the following month for two prototypes (46-525 and 46-526). A mock-up inspection during mid-1946 brought some changes including a 40 degree sweep on the root intakes, which now had a boundary-layer ramp to assist with pressure recovery, and replacement of the V-tail with a conventional layout and high-mounted horizontal surfaces to avoid efflux impact. The design had originally displayed straight wings but the advantages of a swept configuration prevailed and it was to have an ejection seat. The final design was accepted on 14 February 1947, when McDonnell received a formal contract.

The XF-88 made its first flight on 20 October 1948 at the hands of test pilot Robert M Edholm and over tests proved it to be a capable and adequate aircraft but, as with so many of these early jet-powered fighters, the speed was disappointing. For the XF-88 however, it proved inadequate when compared to the F-84 and the F-86. In an attempt to increase performance, the J34-WE-22 with a thrust of 3,600lb (16kN) and short afterburners was installed in the second prototype which made its first flight on 26 April 1949. These engines gave it a slightly higher speed but the additional fuel for power boost negated its value as a long-range escort fighter.

When flight trials were completed the Air Force gave McDonnell indications that it wanted to place it in production and the company planned to install Westinghouse J46 engines with a thrust of 3,980lb (17.7kN) to provide a further improvement in speed. But tight financial constraints and a policy change brought cancellation of the XF-88 in August 1950. Yet the aircraft did have a truly unique place in aviation history. Modified as a high-speed propeller research aircraft and fitted with an Allison XT-35-A-5 turboprop engine in the nose, for which the nose leg had to be relocated to one side, the first prototype was redesignated XF-88B and began flight trials on 14 April 1953 from Langley Field,

Repurposed into a research project for dual propulsion with a turboprop engine in the nose and a single J34 jet in the fuselage, the XF-88 was a precursor to the F-101 Voodoo. (USAF)

Virginia. It was able to achieve just over Mach 1 in a dive, thus becoming the first turboprop-powered aircraft in the world to exceed the speed of sound.

Table 15: McDonnell XF-88 Voodoo Specifications

	XF-88
Span	39.66ft/12.0m
Length	54.08ft/16.48m
Height	17.25ft/5.25m
Empty weight	12,140lb/5,506kg
Gross weight	18,500lb/8,391kg
Max speed	706mph/1,135kph
Ceiling	39,400ft/12,009m
Range	1,737mls/2,794km

Republic XF-91; First Flight: 9 May 1949

This one owes its origin to the prolific array of information about rocket-powered aircraft retrieved from Germany at the end of the Second World War. As a result of that research, Alexander Kartvelli began work on the possibility of a rocket-powered interceptor in 1946 and based a lot of his ideas on the Me 163 Komet. To counter the disadvantage of a short flight duration and extremely limited range, he chose a conventional turbojet engine for normal flight with a rocket motor for high-speed interception and for providing extra speed during combat.

The basic fuselage was a development of that from the F-84 and Kartvelli selected a 5,200lb (23.13kN) General Electric J47-GE-3 turbojet engine and a four-chamber, 13,000lb (57.8kN) Curtiss-Wright XLR27 rocket motor. Two of the four rocket motors were located above the jet tailpipe and two below. The all-new, 35 degree swept wing carried an internal pivot for the pilot to control the angle of incidence which could be varied between -2 degrees and +6 degrees and carried the unusual feature of being broader in chord at the tip than at the root. It was a novel concept, an attempt to reduce the wing's tendency to stall at slow speeds while reducing drag at the wing/fuselage juncture.

Republic faced several structural challenges because of the very thin wing section and the fact that the sweep started at the centreline rather than the more conventional dog-leg design with a straight intersection. There was virtually no stress analysis available on this type of wing and a half-scale box beam was prepared and tested while examining different methods for incurring least weight. As well as the inverse taper, the variable-incidence wing was to provide a powerful means of trim control in both transonic and supersonic flight. This feature had particular advantages for lateral stability, when the inclination of the wing was adjusted to line up the fuselage with the wind flow to compensate. In addition, boosted flight controls were provided, although these were not fitted to the rudder because deflections of this surface are relatively minor at high speeds.

The need for wingtip fuel tanks was driven by the range requirement but unstable air loads they invoked fed large twisting moments to the wings themselves, necessitating the attachment of tank fins. It was discovered that the required size to offset this effect was appreciably less than that required under free air conditions. Nevertheless, Republic conducted a great amount of work to understand the overall effect as well as on the trajectory of the tanks when they were jettisoned so as to ensure clean separation without colliding with the structure.

The landing gear was unusual in that the main legs of the tricycle undercarriage carried two bogies in tandem with retraction outwards so that the wheels were stowed close to the wing tips, a configuration which allowed drop tanks or underwing ordnance to be carried inboard. The overall design did have a legacy in that the swept wing became standard on the production F-84F Thunderstreak (see Volume 4).

The Air Force liked the concept and ordered two XF-91 prototypes (46-680 and 46-681), which Republic named Thunderceptor, maintaining the prefix 'Thunder' which the company had used for its P-47 Thunderbolt. In tests prior to flight, the rocket motors proved excessively troublesome and were replaced with a four-chamber Reaction Motors XLR-11 with a total thrust of 6,000lb (27kN) from four chambers. This was the chosen power for the Bell X-1 transonic research aircraft and had been adopted for several other research and experimental programmes. Each barrel of the four were independently operated and the configuration required all four chambers to be placed in a bulbous enclosure on the underside of the aft fuselage.

Another aircraft with a dual propulsion system. The XF-91 had a J47 turbojet engine and an XLR27 rocket motor but the type failed to satisfy requirements despite some significant changes to the configuration. (USAF)

Rollout occurred on 24 February 1949 and the first flight took place on 9 May with Carl Bellinger at the controls, initial flights using only the turbojet engine. These were followed by flights using reheat and then with rocket power, the first US aircraft to go supersonic in level flight and before the North American F-100. With all engines running, the Thunderceptor could reach Mach 1.71, or 1,126mph (1,811km/hr).

The first prototype was fitted with a radome nose, the intake being relocated to the underside of the radome, while the second aircraft got a butterfly tail. But there were moments of sheer drama, such as the day the engine flamed out and could not be restarted, leaving the XLR-11 rocket motors to bring the Thunderceptor home to Edwards AFB. Testing did prove satisfactory and it received high marks with the expectation of a production order but the aircraft was simply too advanced in its concept, engineering and operability to risk production. With the project cancelled, the second aircraft was relegated to the USAF museum at Wright-Patterson AFB.

Table 16: Republic XF-91 Specifications

	XF-91
Span	31.22ft/9.51m
Length	43.25ft/13.18m
Height	18.09ft/5.51m
Empty weight	15,853lb/7,191kg
Gross weight	18,600lb/8,437kg
Max speed	984mph/1,584kph
Ceiling	55,000ft/16,764m
Range	1,171mls/1,884km

Lockheed XF-90; First Flight: 3 June 1949

The story of Lockheed's bid against the McDonnell XF-88 began in 1946 when project engineers Don Palmer and Bill Ralston started work on the Model 090-32-01, with a contract from the AAF awarded on 20 June for two prototypes (46-687 and 46-688). The same team had been responsible for the P-80 and sifted test and wind tunnel results to inform a burgeoning series of ideas at Lockheed. Over the next year a wide range of concept studies emerged, more than 65 different designs including some extraordinary and bizarre configurations.

Unleashed from the conservative practices of war production, Lockheed's design team came up with butterfly tails, W-shaped wings (the outer panels swept forwards), tri-engine configurations with engines on the wingtips and one in the vertical tail, and some that were simplified down to a single engine mounted in the fuselage and clean, thin and swept wings. At the time the AAF was searching for an optimum specification to satisfy the requirement for a penetration fighter both as a bomber escort and for ground-attack roles.

The basic requirement resulted in a rapidly changing list of specifications, at one time stipulating a combat range of up to 1,500 miles (2,413km) with time-to-height requirements of up to 50,000ft (15,140m) in less than five minutes. But these specifications were fluid and moved up and down according to redefined operational requirements occurring at frequent intervals. Taking a broad approach, the Lockheed team decided not to be overly ambitious and to optimise maximum performance around available engines. They came up with Model 090-32-01 for which on 20 June 1946 the company received a contract for two prototypes (46-687 and 46-688).

At first, basing a lot of their initial work on German research results, the team designed a delta-wing configuration but reversed that decision after wind tunnel tests proved it to be impractical for the multi-role requirement. That forced compromise and the judgement favoured a simplified design with a slender fuselage and pointed nose and 35-degree sweptback wings. Power would be provided by two 3,000lb (13.34kN) thrust axial-flow Westinghouse J34 turbojet engines, mounted side-by-side in the slender fuselage fed by lateral intakes. It had leading-edge slats, Fowler flaps and ailerons on the trailing edge and the pressurised cockpit incorporated an ejection seat beneath the bubble canopy. For combat the XF-90, as it was designated, would carry six 20mm cannon, high-velocity rockets and a bomb load of 2,000lb (907kg) with range extended by wingtip tanks.

To satisfy stress levels for the ground-attack role, the XF-90 was to be fabricated primarily in 75ST aluminium for 15 percent greater strength than the more standard 24ST over heavy forgings and machined parts. But that increased the empty weight to about 50 percent greater than its rival, the McDonnell XF-88 and that low power/weight ratio virtually sealed its fate. This would not be the first time that a requirement

Experimenting with a more stable wing configuration, Alexander Kartvelli chose a novel profile with which the pilot could alter the angle of incidence in flight on a planform which had a wider tip chord than that at the fuselage juncture. (USAF)

The second aircraft (right) got a butterfly tail and the first received a modified nose section incorporating a radome. (USAF)

combining interception and fighter roles with ground-attack duty doomed a design compromised by a multi-role concept.

The first flight of the first prototype took place on 3 June 1949 with Tony LeVier at the controls but, although putting up a credible show, it was too slow and sluggish due to the overweight condition. To improve performance, the second prototype was assigned the afterburning J34-WE-15 with a wet thrust of 4,200lb (18.7kN), designated XF-90A and this demonstrated a speed of 668mph (1,075km/hr) in level flight and Mach 1.12 in a dive. This was the first USAF jet equipped with afterburner and the first Lockheed project to exceed Mach 1 but an assessment judged it inferior to the F-86 which had already been in service for several years.

Lockheed worked up three alternative configurations with different engines including one with a single Allison J33-A-29 (Model 190-33-02), one with two Westinghouse J34-WE-2 engines (Model 290-34-03) or with a single General Electric J47-GE-21 engine (Model 390-35-02) but all options would have required substantial redesign of the fuselage and there was little value in that. The programme was abandoned in September 1950.

Table 17: Lockheed XF-90 Specifications

	XF-90
Span	40ft/12.19m
Length	56.16ft/17.11m
Height	15.75ft/4.8m
Empty weight	18,050lb/8,187kg
Gross weight	27,200kg/12,337kg
Max speed	665mph/1,069kph
Ceiling	39,000ft/11,887m
Range	2,300mls/3,700km

Designed to meet the requirement for a long-range penetration fighter, the XF-90 was the first Air Force jet with afterburner and used exotic new metals but it failed to satisfy. (USAF)

North American YF-93; First Flight: 24 January 1950

Justification for including this type, which made its first flight beyond the cut-off date for this volume, is the relevance it has to other projects of the late 1940s. Competing to the same requirement as McDonnell with the XF-88 and Lockheed with the XF-90, North American was a little later with its YF-93 which began as an in-house project designated NA-157 in late 1947.

In some respects it was a development of the F-86A in that it adopted the same swept wing and tail assembly but displayed a completely new fuselage and engine. The engine selected was the Pratt & Whitney J48-P-6 with a dry thrust of 6,000lb (26.69kN) and a wet thrust of 8,750lb (38.92kN), a US version of the Rolls-Royce RB.44 Tay which was a development of the Nene. Much larger than the J47 in the F-86A, it necessitated a wider and longer fuselage. With a high internal fuel capacity, the weight of the aircraft required a twin-wheel unit for each main landing leg.

Recognising the heritage connection to the F-86A, the Air Force ordered two prototypes in December 1947 (48-317 and 48-318) and had applied the designation F-86C, with six 20mm cannon and 225 rounds per gun. It also had an SCR-720 search radar which forced relocation of the intake to two NACA-designed ear-shaped intakes either side of the fuselage, each aircraft having a slightly different intake shape. The Air Force was sold on the F-86C before flight but because of the major reconfiguration decided it was to be designated YF-93A. If it performed well there was expectation that it would be ordered into production and in fact an order for 118 aircraft was lodged with North American.

Before completion of the two prototypes, the programme was cancelled in February 1949 due to the outstanding performance of the Boeing B-47 which displayed a capability to go it alone through denied airspace. By this date the requirement for a dedicated penetration fighter and long-range escort that had driven the XF-88 and the XF-90 was redundant. The introduction of the new all-jet bombers caused a radical rethink on how fighters would be used in future, the extended range and high speed of these aircraft driving a change in policy and the tactical deployment of offensive power. But that was only one reason. The year-on-year reduction of defence budgets was taking its toll and there were insufficient funds for everything the Air Force would have liked.

NAA test pilot George Welch took the YF-9A into the air for the first time on 24 January 1950, with the fly-off between the three contenders during the summer. The USAF Evaluation Board selected the XF-88 as the winner and the other two were dropped. As noted, the XF-88 never did make it into service as all procurement contracts now focused on production of existing types for the Korean War. The two prototypes were tested by the NACA and used extensively in evaluation comparisons with the later century-series fighters of the 1950s, before they were scrapped in 1956.

Table 18: North American YF-93 Specifications

	YF-93A
Span	38.75ft/11.81m
Length	44.08ft/13.43m
Height	15.66ft/4.77m
Empty weight	14,035lb/6,366kg
Gross weight	21,610lb/9,802kg
Max speed	708mph/1,139kph
Ceiling	46,800ft/14,264m
Range	2,000mls/3,218km

Developed during the late 1940s as an escort fighter, the YF-93 succumbed to the redundant requirement made obsolete by the introduction of the B-47, a fast, all-jet medium bomber. (USAF)

A NOTE ON HISTORICAL SOURCES

The source material for these volumes originates from primary references and peer-reviewed historical reports and analyses which, over the ensuing decades since the events from which they were compiled took place, have been re-examined with the additional advantage of access to declassified material and further investigation.

Here, a concerted effort has been made not to use the work of aviation writers past or present for reference. The vast majority of recognised aviation and aeronautical historians provide valued material in books or articles and their work can be a useful resource for the armchair enthusiast and active hobbyist as well as for the professional historian. Moreover, there are now many specialised internet-based resources embracing special-interest-groups (SIGs) to encourage further exchange of information.

However, a very few writers, usually known within the fraternity of aviation historians and pressured by deadlines and delivery dates, use regurgitated text which can be flawed or too generalised to warrant credible repetition. In almost all instances, verification is key to establishing fact from speculation or assumption and that can be a time-consuming activity which demand high levels of commitment.

In studying the history of US air power, a general and readily accessible resource is the Air Force Historical Foundation which has a peer-reviewed journal issued four times each year with numerous articles and special features directing attention to specific events, theatres of engagement or equipment. It is a valued and highly respected source for initial contact with events and activities throughout the period covered by these volumes.

Also of great use is the Air University at Maxwell AFB, Alabama, and the Air University Press, which is the academic publisher of the US Air Force. Together, their publicly available materials have provided the author with reliable and verified information. In addition, the US Department of Defense, the Air Force Historical Support Division, the Historical Office of the Secretary of Defense, the Naval History and Heritage Command and the US National Archives were visited and consulted during a professional association over many decades. Collectively, they have provided material from which these volumes are compiled.

On the recording of inventories, it is noted that individual units and commands were not always accurate in the numbers of aircraft claimed to be on strength and in some cases there were attempts to raise quotas artificially, little discrimination being made as to aircraft assigned versus those operationally available, factors which vary day by day. There are also variations in performance figures quoted in numerous official reports for specific types of aircraft. Aircraft performance is much argued over by amateur and professional historians.

To be specific for instance, there is no 'maximum speed' for a particular aircraft type, except that defined as an engineering or atmospheric limit on structural stress or capability. Speed varies according to load, altitude, fuel levels and variations in engine performance, all variables which skew the recorded values. In these volumes, the USAF Standard Aircraft Characteristics charts have been used to show the equivalent values for realistic comparison between types but here too there are variations which affect performance levels of individual aircraft.

Supplementing military histories and the various official unit command diaries are manufacturers' logs and production records. Here, the annual yearbooks of The Aircraft Industries Association of America for the chronological periods in question proved invaluable for obtaining annual data from which has been drawn production numbers and various engineering developments and achievements. The individual manufacturers also provided archival material from which events and activities were reconstructed.

For specific contextual alignment between events and the period within which they occurred, an invaluable asset is the digitisation of every issue of *Aviation Week*, the aviation trade journal for which every issue since it was first published in 1916 is available for subscribers to their platform. It is within such coverage that transient and inconsequential events and activities can add perspective or context.

Other periodicals and journals are less readily available in print form but if they can be found they are frequently a valuable resource for detailed accounts of little-known events. One valued and highly accessible organisation is the American Aviation Historical Society. It publishes a journal which covers both civil and military US aviation from its earliest days to the recent past and frequently records the experiences of individuals and organisations. Digital subscribers can access every issue for reference.

The content of the *US Air Power 1945–1990* series comes from all of the above and the author's files compiled through access to numerous organisations, government departments, company archives, learned societies and academic institutions across 60 years of professional involvement, with the help and assistance of individuals and respected aviation historians around the world. All of which to whom the author is indebted.

BIBLIOGRAPHY

Anderson, F, *Northrop, An Aeronautical History* (Century City, California: Northrop Corporation, 1976)

Andrade, J. M., *U.S. Military Designations and Serials 1909-1979* (Midland Countries Publications, 1997)

Bilstein, R. E., *Orders of Magnitude, A History of the NACA and NASA 1915-1990* SP-4406 (Washington DC, National Aeronautics and Space Administration, 1989)

Bowers, Peter M., *Boeing Aircraft since 1916* (Putnam Aeronautical Books, 1989)

Bowers, Peter M., *Curtiss Aircraft 1907-1947* (Putnam & Company Ltd, 1979)

Bridgman, L (ed), *Jane's All the World Aircraft 1948-49* (Jane's Publishing, 1948); *Jane's All the World's Aircraft 1949-50* (Jane's Publishing, 1949)

Bright, Charles D., *The Jet Makers: The Aerospace Industry from 1945 to 1972* (The Regents Press of Kansas, 1978)

Buttler, Tony, *American Secret Projects: Fighters and Interceptors 1945-1976* (Midland Publishing, 2007)

Dawson, V. P., *Engines and Innovation: Lewis Laboratory and American Propulsion Technology* (Schiffer Publishing, 1991)

Francillon, Rene J., *Lockheed Aircraft since 1913* (Putnam & Company, 1982)

Francillon, Rene J., *McDonnell Douglas Aircraft since 1920* (Putnam & Company, 1979)

Frisbee, John L., *Makers of the United States Air Force* (Air Force History and Museums Program, 1996)

Goldberg, Alfred, *A History of the United States Air Force* (Arno Press, 1957)

Hansen, J. R., *Engineer in Charge, A History of the Langley Aeronautical Laboratory 1917-1958* SP-4305 (Washington DC, National Aeronautics and Space Administration, 1987)

Hartman, E. P., *Adventures in Research, A History of Ames Research Center 1940-1965* SP-4302 (Washington DC, National Aeronautics and Space Administration, 1970)

Jenkins, D. R., and Landis, T. R., *Experimental & Prototype U.S. Air Force Jet Fighters* (Specialty Press, 2008)

Kay, A. L., *Turbojet, History & Development 1930-1960 Volume 2* (Crowood Press, 2007)

Knaack, M. S., *Encyclopedia of US Air Force Aircraft and Missile Systems Volume I: Post-World War II Fighters 1945-1973* (Office of Air Force History, 1978)

Loftin, L. F., Jr., *Quest for Performance, The Evolution of Modern Aircraft*, SP-468 (Washington DC, National Aeronautics and Space Administration, 1985)

Matthews, B., *Cobra! Bell Aircraft Corporation 1934-1946* (Schiffer, 1976)

Neufeld, J. (ed), *Research and Development in the United States Air Force* (Center for Air Force History, United States Air Force, 1993)

Neufeld, J., Watson, G. M. Jr., and Chenoweth, D. (ed), *Technology and the Air Force, a Retrospective Assessment* (Air Force History and Museums Program, 1997)

Norton, Bill, *American Aircraft Development World War Two Legacy 1945-1953 and The Korean War* (Fonthill Media Ltd, 2021)

Patillo, Donald M., *Pushing the Envelope: The American Aircraft Industry* (The University of Michigan Press, 1998)

Rae, John B., *Climb to Greatness: The American Aircraft Industry 1920-1960* (The MIT Press, 1968)

Rubinstein, M., and Goldman R. M., *To Join with the Eagles: A Complete History of Curtiss-Wright Aircraft from 1903 to 1965* (Doubleday & Company, 1974)

Stoff, J., *The Thunder Factory, An Illustrated History of the Republic Aviation Corporation* (Motorbooks International, 1990)

Swanborough G., and Bowers, P. M., *United States Military Aircraft since 1909* (Putnam Aeronautical Books, 1989)

White, Graham, *R-2800 Pratt & Whitney's Dependable Masterpiece* (Airlife Publishing Ltd, 2001)

White, Graham, *R-4360 Pratt & Whitney's Major Miracle* (Specialty Press, 2006)

ABOUT THE AUTHOR

Born to an RAF family in England toward the end of the Second World War, the author has had a professional career within aerospace, working with NASA, the US Air Force and aviation manufacturers before becoming a professional aerospace historian and writer. Elected to the International Academy of Astronautics, David has also received: the Rolls-Royce Award for the Best Propulsion Submission, RAeS Aerospace Journalist of the Year Awards 1998; the Arthur C Clarke Award (2005); and the American Astronautical Society's Frederick I Ordway Award (2017) presented at the NASA Marshall Space Flight Center. During the 1980s, David was managing director if his aerospace consulting company with offices in London and Princeton, New Jersey. He has been editor of *Horizons*, the house magazine of the former Smith's Industries, two Jane's yearbooks, *Aviation News* and *SpaceFlight* magazine. Apart from aerospace, David is interested in geopolitics, the history of twentieth century warfare, film and classical music, when he is not engaging with the natural world with his wife Ann.